BECOMING WOMEN OF WORTH

Stories of Sugar N' Spice and Recipes for the Holidays

KRISTEN CLARK

KRISTEN CLARK

Published by American Mutt Press, a division of The Communication Leader, LLC.

The publisher gratefully acknowledges the many individuals who granted American Mutt Press permission to print and reprint all materials.

Edited by Kristen Clark with American Mutt Press.

Front cover photo courtesy of Shutterstock, Inc., image ID 318838628.

Back cover photo of Kristen Clark courtesy of Lawrence J. Clark.

AMERICAN MUTT PRESS
Copyright © 2015

ISBN-13: 978-1943470037
ISBN-10: 1943470030

Contents

Recipes

Get the 1ˢᵗ THREE Chapters Free!

So, whether you eat or drink, or whatever you do,
do all to the glory of God.

1 Corinthians 10:31 (ESV)

A Few Special Words

Kristen Clark

And wine to gladden the heart of man,
oil to make his face shine and bread to strengthen man's heart.
Psalm 104:15 (ESV)

As we head toward my favorite time of the year – Christmas - I am already smelling gingerbread and pumpkin spice. That's right, the holiday seasons always seem close at hand and that means opportunities for baked goods and breads.

Instantly, I'm reminded of the Proverbs Woman, noted for rising in the middle of the night to prepare food for her household. Just imagine the smells that might have wafted through the night air in her home. I envision bread made for strengthening a man's heart (Psalm 104:15) and delicious baked goods made of the kind of herbs that grow in the midst of deep love (Proverbs 15:17). Yum!

I'm also reminded of the many bake-offs that take place throughout the year, what I call emotional rollercoasters as some participants proudly take home a blue ribbon while others walk away in tears, beaten by time and perfectionism. Yes, baking can be rewarding and equally frustrating at the same time.

Most importantly, I'm reminded of the many women who've become special friends over the breaking of bread (Acts 2:42). And I celebrate the personal exchange of experience, strength, and hope that has taken place over the sharing of tried and true recipes.

This book is the third in the *Women of Worth* series and a celebration of all that is embodied in the sugar and spice of baking. It is a tribute to the role baked goods play:

- In relationships with our families and loved ones
- In the memories of our traditions and culture
- In our efforts at service and accomplishment

It is also a tribute to the attitudes and practices that help us develop thoughts about ourselves that are as precious as God's thoughts are about us. When we bake for others we indulge in discipline, practice, bravery, and creativity - mindsets also required for embracing our role as Women of Worth.

The stories featured in this book are symbolic of these mindsets and touch on the same struggles in perfection, disappointment, and adversity. They also illustrate the joy and blessing of serving others and the reward of the hard work that goes into making a dish worthy of a blue ribbon.

As I read these stories the first time, I laughed and cried equally. More importantly, I remembered why we strive as hard as we do in the kitchen. I remembered that starting and completing a task is one way we validate ourselves. When we do well in creating a dish worthy of consumption and praise, we feel good about ourselves. We inherently feel a sense of accomplishment and we take delight in that accomplishment. We also learn to laugh at our mistakes and press on. In this way, we grow. We evolve. We reach a higher level of contentment with self. Ultimately, we rediscover what we already know about ourselves but are sometimes slow to embrace or quick to forget – that we are Women of Worth.

Enjoy! And happy baking!

*Go then, eat your bread in happiness
and drink your wine with a cheerful heart;
for God has already approved your works.*

Ecclesiastes 9:7 (NASB)

Lessons From My Bread Basket

Sally Ferguson

How many loaves do you have?
Mark 6:38 (NIV)

What is it that makes bread such a treat? Here are a few of my favorite things!

Aroma

The aroma of rising sourdough fills my senses. Mixed scents of yeast, sugar and flour blend together in a comfort-food-kind-of-way. For ten years, I baked loaves of sourdough. The starter's constant need for babysitting was time consuming, yet yielded mouth-watering slices. Regardless of the type of bread, and the process the beginning stage held, the smell always made me feel wrapped in the comforts of home. Maybe that's why Paul said I am the aroma of Christ (2 Corinthians 2:14-16). When a believer wraps someone in love, they experience a homecoming too; an unconditional acceptance that says, "I'm glad you're here."

Taste

The aroma goes hand-in-hand with taste, because taste buds are triggered by a sense of smell and connect me to memories associated with that fragrance. Taste buds have sensors indicating sweet, sour and salty differences. When I bite into cornbread made with honey, I'm transported to that sunny picnic at the family reunion. Strawberry Nut Bread brings to mind summer trips to the strawberry patch with my kids in tow. Rye Bread has a hearty-nutty wholesomeness. But none of these breads can be completely sampled on aroma alone. No, a bite into crunchy crust unpacks another level of connection with the bread experience. And it's also true in my walk with the Lord. It can't be a hands-off relationship where I stand back and observe. Psalm 34:8 says, "Taste and see that the Lord is good."

Process

Kneading the dough is a sensory experience involving touch, smell and sight. Pushing and pulling the dough releases pent-up frustrations and sooths the mind. The steady rhythm makes the dough more pliable as it strengthens the gluten strands. When ready, oil is used to prevent a crust forming during the rising stage. Isn't that what I need, too? The oil of the Holy Spirit keeps me pliable in God's hands. He forms and shapes me into a loaf that nourishes others. (Psalm 23:5)

The process of grinding flour "is done with steel or stone rollers that break the wheat kernels, then grind the pieces to a fine flour."[1] Does that ever remind me of the grinding process in my own character, as the Lord breaks down my pride and the attributes that detract from what He wants to build in my life! I also have to break down the things that separate me from others, so we can be one in Christ. (Ephesians 4:2-3)

Sustenance

Another one of bread's great qualities is the way it fills me up. The properties of flour, sugar, salt, eggs, leavening agents and liquids combine a satisfying content. I've concocted all kinds of breads: with cheese, garlic, apples, buttermilk, herbs, blueberries, molasses, cranberries, almonds, oatmeal, chives and zucchini. But my family always gobbles up Banana Nut Bread the fastest. Breads nourish hunger. People can survive on bread and water alone!

God's Word gives reminders of His sufficiency. He provided manna for the traveling Israelites, and He supplies my daily portion (Psalm 105:40; Lamentations 3:24). David reminds me in Psalm 119:57 that nothing else can fill the longing in my heart. Ecclesiastes 3:11 says God has set eternity in my heart – that void that only He can fill. And then Jesus came and fulfilled that void by saying, "I am the Bread of Life." (John 6:35)

Breaking Bread Together

Remember the disciples breaking bread together in Acts 2:42-47? Because they ate meals in community, they nourished each other physically. Emotionally, they grew as family, in that bond developed in the process of spending time together.

Over the years, many women became special friends over shared bread! I got my first sourdough starter from Maggie and took it when we moved from Indiana to Missouri. There, I exchanged recipes with my new friend, Charlotte. She encouraged me to use starter in recipes that called for hot roll mix, and thus expanded my repertoire of sweet breads. We fostered a kinship over fresh bread and were gratified to provide treats for our families. The starter moved again with me to New York, where my neighbor's daughter dubbed it "Fergy Bread." Other friends have passed along starter from Amish Friendship Bread, so appropriately named because the sharing of bread fosters friendship!

Heritage

The legacy of good cooks is passed on from generation to generation. Having a recipe from my Mom, Gra'ma, or even from a beloved friend is like welcoming them into my own kitchen once again. Fond memories bring back conversations around the dinner table, where steaming plates of food nourished and filled us. We invest in each other's lives by spending time together and affirming life's seasons. The Proverbs 31 Woman was celebrated for the way she provided for her family throughout the seasons of her life (Proverbs 31:15). I like thinking I am leaving a legacy for my children, with traditions of cherished family recipes. My inheritance as a believer, is a hope that will never spoil.

My Heavenly Father longs to feed and care for His own. Naomi received news that the Lord had provided food for her homeland, and so she returned with her daughter-in-law, Ruth (Ruth 1:6). In Proverbs 30:8, Agur said my daily bread comes from the Lord. I am constantly amazed at the ways the Lord meets my needs and fills me to overflowing. He is my Provider.

The aroma and taste of bread fill the senses. As I sink my teeth into the savory flavors, the Lord nourishes me with the sustenance of His Word, so that I can feed others with the loaves I have received!

(1) Sharon Tyler Herbst, <u>Breads</u> (Tucson: HP Books, 1983), p. 5.

Sally Ferguson is an author and speaker. She lives in the rolling hills of western New York with her husband and her dad. She has a daughter, son, daughter-in-love & two of the world's most precious granddaughters! Sally's coloring book, What Will I Be When I Grow Up?, and her ebook, How to Plan a Women's Retreat, are both available on Amazon. Stop in for a chat at www.sallyferguson.net.

For He has satisfied the thirsty soul,
and the hungry soul He has filled with what is good.

Psalm 107:9 (NASB)

Bread in a Bag

My daughter won a Blue Ribbon at the State Fair with this recipe!

Ingredients:

- 2 c all-purpose flour
- 1 pkg rapid rise yeast
- 3 T sugar
- 3 T nonfat dry milk
- dash salt
- 1 c hot water
- 3 T oil
- 1 c whole wheat flour

Directions:

Mix 1 cup all-purpose flour with yeast, sugar, milk, and salt in a 1 gallon freezer bag. Force out air, seal, and blend with fingers.

Add oil and water. Mix.

Add whole wheat flour and enough all-purpose flour to make stiff firm dough. Knead.

Add more flour as needed. Knead two to four minutes. Shape in ball. Let rest in bag ten minutes.

Split bag open and roll dough into 12 x 7 rectangle. Roll back into cylinder shape and pinch ends to seal. Place in greased loaf pan (8½ x 4½ x 2¼), rotate to grease bread.

Cover with plastic.

Fill another pan halfway with boiling water. Set loaf pan on top with rack and let rise 20 minutes.

Bake in preheated oven, 375 degrees for 25–30 minutes.

Yes, The Process Matters

Dorothy Hill

Give us this day our daily bread.
Matthew 6:11 (AMP)

Bread Matters

The smell of baking bread almost makes me hyperventilate. When I inhale slowly and deeply enough to imprint that aroma on my brain, I become lightheaded. Of course, the smell also activates all the salivary glands that churn out saliva to prepare for the chewing and swallowing of this wonderful bread. Yes, I love baking and eating bread.

This recipe did not originate with me. I don't remember if a friend shared it with me, or if I found it online. There are other versions of English Muffin Bread that are close to this one and others that vary a great deal. Someone used the "goopy" word and I liked it a lot, so I included it. It's accurate because the dough *is* goopy. It's memorable and it made me smile. Reading recipes usually does not make me smile. They are pretty pragmatic and most people don't think cooking and baking are a laughing matter.

Reading Matters

It is always a good idea to read completely through the recipe first. Then preheat the oven, get all the ingredients measured and waiting in the order they will be used. It is probably apparent I've forgotten an ingredient or two over the years. And let me tell you, things just don't turn out like you expect them to when that happens. My first attempt making fudge was disastrous. I dumped all the ingredients into the pan and fired up the burner. After it came to a rolling boil I read the directions. After it boiled for a bit I poured it into a buttered pan and hoped for the best. Hoping didn't make it happen. That fudge was harder than concrete. I tried, but couldn't break it with a hammer.

Measuring Matters

My sister-in-law did not put out the measured ingredients in the order they were to be added to her apple pie. That was the dessert for a dinner whose guest of honor was her husband's boss. She was distracted and busy and mixed the apple pie filling. She spooned it into the crust and popped the pie in the oven. Unfortunately, she was on a perennial diet so she didn't taste the apple pie filling mixture. (I've never believed those calories count in the scheme of things because we are testing food and protecting our loved ones.) Imagine her complete dismay and embarrassment when she discovered that instead of cinnamon she put chili powder in the pie. I'm pretty sure it tasted - not like apple pie - even with the ice cream. I don't even know how one apologizes or make amends for such a gastric surprise. Measure your ingredients and set them in order before you, too, serve Chili Apple Pie or some surprise version of your favorite bread.

Eating Matters

English Muffin Bread is best toasted, slathered with a fair amount of butter, and topped with your favorite jam, jelly, or my personal favorite, honey. It makes a fabulous egg sandwich when the yolk is thoroughly cooked… a somewhat messy one when it isn't, but still a good eat. Also makes a terrific BLT (cue the salivary glands).

Gratitude Matters

I am so thankful for the bountiful gift of bread. Having bread with our meal should cause us to remember that Jesus is the Bread of Life. (John 6:48) When Jesus taught the disciples how to pray in Matthew 6:11 it was the first petition He made… "Give us this day our daily bread." He Himself is our provision. Only He can meet the deepest needs of our soul. We have so much for which to be grateful. Thank You, Lord Jesus.

Dorothy Hill and her husband, Jerry, live in Maumelle, AR. She is a retired public school teacher and college associate professor. Currently she teaches a ladies Bible study class. Dorothy has had poetry published in Christian Single Magazine and is currently writing a book on adoption with her daughter, Terri. She blogs at www.dorothysdesk.com where she offers a bit of encouragement.

So Abraham hurried into the tent to Sarah,
and said, "Quickly, prepare three measures of fine flour,
knead it and make bread cakes."

Genesis 18:6 (NASB)

English Muffin Bread

Ingredients:

- 5 ½ cups flour
- 2 tablespoons dry yeast
- 1-2 tablespoons honey
- ¼ cup warm water
- 2 teaspoons kosher salt
- ¼ teaspoon baking powder
- 2 ¼ cups warm whole milk
- Butter and cornmeal for greasing and dusting the pans

Directions:

Butter the loaf pans and dust each with about 1 T. cornmeal. Set aside.

Mix the yeast, honey, and water. Set aside.

Sift the salt, baking powder, and flour.

Add the milk and one cup of the flour to the yeast mixture. Blend well.

Add the remaining flour and mix well. You should have a very soft, goopy dough. (Yes. I said goopy.)

Spoon the dough into the 2 prepared loaf pans. Set aside in a warm place until the batter has doubled and is at the top of the pans, or a little above.

Preheat the oven to 425F.

Dust the tops of the loaves with cornmeal and bake for 15 minutes or so. The loaf will sound hollow when tapped. Bake for 20-25 minutes if you want a crisper, more golden crust.

Cool and slice.

This bread is best toasted and served with butter and honey.

Yield: 2 loaves.

There Just Is No Substitute

Kristen Clark

*Jesus answered, "I am the way and the truth and the life. No one
comes to the Father except through me."*
John 14:6 (NIV)

"Kris, does this look familiar?"

I stared at the yellowed and lined page, searching my
mind for some memory. "Maybe," I said. "Is this my
writing?"

Mom giggled, "Yes."

I turned the page over to read the front of it and saw the
title. "Oh, yes, I remember these!" I smiled widely. "I
used to love making these."

I held the aged paper in my hands and read the
ingredients for what I remembered being the first dessert
I ever made as a child. Church Window Cookies!

I was a girl when I brought home the recipe from my
home-economics class, and I couldn't wait to try it out.
Mom bought the ingredients for me and sat at the
kitchen counter observing the process, just in case I ran
into problems. A sugary aroma infused the kitchen as I
stirred the melting butter, vanilla extract, chopped

walnuts, and chocolate chips in a sauce pan. After folding in the colored marshmallows, I rolled out the mixture into logs and coated them with coconut flakes.

"I don't like coconut," my little sister announced as she watched the process.

"More for me," I said in my best condescendingly big-sister voice.

After chilling the coconut-coated logs in the fridge for a few hours, I sliced the treats into thin wafers, letting each slice fall open onto the cookie sheet. I loved how the colored marshmallows resembled the stained glass in church windows and reminded me of Christmas.

Mom interrupted my trip down memory lane, "When was the last time you made Church Window Cookies?"

I laughed. Truth is, I don't do much cooking as an adult. God has blessed me with a husband who excels in this area and he does 95% of the grocery shopping and cooking at our house. And, we eat like kings.

Then Mom reminded me of the time I wanted to make brownies from a box one day after school. She was visiting the neighbor next door when I stopped by to tell her of my plans to make brownies. She said I could.

When she returned home after her visit, she asked how the brownies turned out.

"Great," I said.

"Did we have everything you needed?"

"Yes, except for one ingredient. But I found a substitute," I said in a matter of fact tone.

"A substitute?" she asked.

"Uh huh. We didn't have any vegetable oil, so I found this bottle to use instead." It was the same color as the vegetable oil we usually used, so I thought it would be just fine.

It was then I learned that White Karo syrup was NOT a substitute for vegetable oil!

I shook my head, "Did I really do that?"

"You and your sister thought those brownies were terrific. But they were too chewy and sweet for me and your dad." Mom continued, "After that, I paid closer attention to what we had on hand for ingredients, just in case you thought you might substitute something else sometime."

Mom and I laughed over the memories of my limited baking experiences. Her story about the brownies made me think about how there are also no substitutes when it comes to my faith. Jesus is the way, the truth, and the life (John 14:6). No one comes to the Father except through Him, and that's when I remembered why I love the idea of the Church Window Cookies; there is nothing that speaks of Grace and Mercy like the love Jesus has for His church.

Kristen Clark, award-winning author, speaker, and coach, is a real-life example of someone who conquered low self-esteem by developing confidence as a spiritual mindset. Her articles have appeared in numerous journals and magazines, while her inspirational short stories have been published in Chicken Soup for the Soul and other compilation books. A member of the American Association of Christian Counselors, her book, Becoming a Woman of Worth: Creating a More Confident You won the Gold medal in Christian Biblical Counseling in the 2014 Readers' Favorite International Book Contest. Feel free to visit www.HisSideoftheLookingGlass.com for more information.

Church Window Cookies

Prep time: 10 minutes
Cooking time: 5 minutes
Ready in: 75 minutes

Ingredients:

- ½ cup butter
- 1 teaspoon vanilla extract
- 1 cup chopped walnuts
- 1 16 oz package colored miniature marshmallows
- 2 cups flaked coconut
- 1 16 oz package milk chocolate chips

Directions:

Melt butter and chocolate chips in a heavy saucepan over medium heat; mix until smooth and creamy; remove from heat and stir in the vanilla. Fold in the marshmallows and walnuts.

Scatter half of the coconut onto a large baking sheet. Form the chocolate mixture into two oblong logs and lay them onto the coconut. Use the remaining coconut to coat the logs.

Refrigerate until the logs are firm, about 1 hour. Cut logs into 3/4-inch slices and serve.

A sated man loathes honey,
But to a famished man any bitter thing is sweet.

Proverbs 27:7 (NASB)

A Legacy of Hospitality

Dorothy Johnson

*They broke bread in their homes
and ate together with glad and sincere hearts,
Acts 2:46b (NIV)*

My mother and daddy loved people and entertained often. Although their efforts weren't elaborate, Mother had a knack for making simple fare special by setting a pretty table. She usually kept a small bouquet of fresh flowers or leaves and berries from our yard as a centerpiece. Even when I was young, she enlisted my help to get ready for guests. I might set the table, stir something on the stove, or dish up individual dessert portions onto her best china. Later, my children got in on the act. Looking back I realize it was good training for when we would entertain in our own homes.

Sometimes the house was filled with relatives, but more often, they'd invite neighbors and friends in for dinner or just dessert and coffee. Whatever the occasion, Mother always baked a confection to serve. However, all her "hostessing" wasn't planned. She welcomed drop-in guests with equal enthusiasm. Daddy had a sweet tooth, so she usually had some kind of dessert on hand to serve. I can still see her bustling around her big kitchen, putting on a fresh pot of coffee and assembling a plate of cookies or cutting slices of pie or cake.

Mother liked to try new recipes and was always on the lookout for something tasty to serve. One of her standard offerings, Nut Pie, dates back to the 1970s. This crust-less wonder features a chewy nutty base—think egg whites, sugar, pecans and graham cracker crumbs—topped with a cloud of whipped cream. It's especially good with coffee in cold weather; although she served it year round.

The only failure with the pie that I know of happened when unexpected company interrupted my Aunt Mary in the middle of mixing one together. I suppose her guests weren't of the sort she felt free to invite into the kitchen while she finished. Once they were gone, she went back and folded the crumb mixture into the egg whites, hoping for the best. Unfortunately, that *best* wasn't so great. I remember her giggles as she told me that pie turned out flat as a flitter. Thank goodness she had time to make another.

Even back when I was a new cook, I could turn out a Nut Pie I was proud to serve. I will confess that I often resorted to Cool Whip in place of real whipped cream. I didn't realize my sacrilege until I served it to two home economic teachers who quizzed me about the topping. These days if you don't want to make your own whipped cream, there are some pretty good aerosol versions available in the dairy section. One important thing to know is that it's good to make this pie the day before because of the 6-hour chilling period. I actually like that idea because that's one job out of the way on the day of the dinner.

Even though my mother normally used her pretty glassware and dishes, I came to recognize what she instinctively understood. Offerings don't have to be served on fancy dinnerware or even be homemade to make guests feel welcome. A drink of cold water and a store-bought cookie offered on disposable plates and cups can be just right when done in the spirit of true hospitality.

With fall upon us, I've been thinking of Mother's tasty Nut Pie. I think I'll make one and invite friends in for a visit. I'll get out some pretty plates and napkins and brew a pot of good coffee. All the while, I'll think of Mother and Daddy and give thanks for what they taught me about the importance of friendship and cordial generosity.

I promise you, my mother's Nut Pie is a great excuse for a little party. It's so easy you might want to stir one up for your own gathering.

Dorothy Johnson and her husband, Terry, live with their three kitties on a ridge overlooking the Arkansas River in Little Rock, Arkansas. The grandmother of eight and a retiree with a background in publishing, Dorothy took up fiction and poetry writing after attending a writers' retreat in 2011. She blogs at Reflections from Dorothy's Ridge. A lover of scripture, she also teaches Bible studies and contributes devotionals and poetry to Alive Now, an Upper Room publication, and FaithHappenings.com. Dorothy is currently working on her first novel, which she describes as a redemption story.

Do we not have a right to eat and drink?

1 Corinthians 9:4 (NASB)

Mother's Nut Pie

Ingredients:

- 3 egg whites
- 1-cup sugar
- ¾ cup Graham Cracker crumbs (5 crackers)
- 1 tsp. baking powder
- 1 tsp. vanilla
- 1 cup chopped pecans
- Dash of salt

Directions:

Beat egg whites until stiff. Add sugar and continue beating until very stiff.

Mix graham cracker crumbs and baking powder. Fold into egg white mixture.

Add vanilla, pecans and salt.

Pour into a greased 9-inch pie pan and bake 30 minutes at 350 degrees.

Chill for 6 hours. Serve with a dollop of whipped cream.

He who gathers in summer is a son who acts wisely,
But he who sleeps in harvest is a son who acts shamefully.

Proverbs 10:5 (NASB)

Confession of a Cook

Laurie Smith

*She was able to make a mess in the kitchen
and set a few small fires.*
Unknown

Growing up a rancher's daughter in Colorado, I can remember huge meals being prepared at cow camp or when branding season was upon us. Friends, neighbors, young and old alike came to help. Hungry cowboys came in for a meal at lunch when a sandwich and chips were nowhere to be found. I learned to cook early on in life because the women that helped raise me were always in the kitchen, cooking, canning, or cutting up deer meat to be wrapped and put away for the winter.

But homemade desserts… well, they were to die for!

We moved to the Lone Star State 25 years ago and that's when I discovered that banana pudding is a staple food item, meant to be eaten at least once a week. It showed up at church socials and family dinners, and almost every restaurant in town had it on their menu. To make a long story short (which mine never are), with all the cooking I had done over the years banana pudding from scratch was something I had never made. But I felt the undue pressure of my church women friends to make this "bowl of heaven" for serving here on earth. It was an unspoken rule: if you live in Texas you should be able to make this delight at the drop of a hat for various occasions, including a simple Saturday night of playing Spades or 42, a baby shower, church fellowship, a funeral, or a "pleased to meet you" dish for a new neighbor. Nope, there was no pressure. None at all.

Well of course I knew how to make pudding from a box, but those savvy church ladies I loved so dearly could spot the "fake stuff" right off! So I set my sights on obtaining a tried and true recipe that someone might be willing to share. That turned out to be no small task as most women are awful funny about sharing their prized family recipe. They say things like, "Well, I've just made it so many times over the years that I kind of eyeball it. You know a little of this and a little of that."

Empty handed, I began searching my own cook books. I tried several recipes, but nothing as rich and creamy as I had tasted. I have always been a firm believer in the freshest and highest quality ingredients one can afford. Since eggs and cream are the main ingredients in banana pudding there are no cutting corners there. And having raised chickens and eaten fresh eggs, once you try them you will never go back to store bought again. So, after several trials and errors, I came up with what I call Mimi's Southern Banana Pudding, (previously called Mom's Banana Pudding before I had grandbabies).

Armed with total confidence and my prettiest vintage turquoise bowl, I proudly set my contribution down at the next church fellowship dinner. I waited anxiously for folks to start sampling MY PUDDING!

I was sure it ranked up there with the seasoned veterans that had been making this dish since they were knee high to a grasshopper! I must confess I knew I had gone overboard with this whole perfect recipe thing but I couldn't help myself. But pride comes before the fall. Old reruns of I Love Lucy came to mind as I gasped in horror at the question I heard asked loud enough for *everyone* to here, "Is THIS Tapioca with nilla wafers in it?"

I couldn't decide if I should just crawl under the table, or quietly walk around the dining hall, snatch up every bowl of pudding that belonged to me, and run for the house! I was in such a hurry that morning when I made the pudding for church that I failed to strain the egg mixture after I tempered it, (that all important step necessary in keeping the pudding smooth and free from pieces of weird rubbery bits hidden in that lovely cream). Yes, folks that day were eating tiny bits of cooked egg whites that I had not separated thoroughly that morning and that had been overcooked in the tempering process!

Why couldn't this have happened to a batch I made at home? At least there, my sweet husband would have simply asked, "Honey, what is this?" No! Instead, this had to happen at a church social! Right in front of God and everybody.

But as I looked around, I saw our friends and family laughing and talking and just simply enjoying being together. That was all that mattered. Those who ate my pudding that day were gracious enough not to mention it again, and we call that good manners in the South.

Otherwise, the day turned out to be a perfect day with not such a perfect desert.

We all show love in different ways, but time spent preparing a meal is a measure of love. Sometimes big meals are happily prepared for dusty ol' cowboys or large family gatherings. Sometimes for life celebrations like weddings and baby showers. Sometimes for a tired new Mom and Dad just home from the hospital with their sweet baby. And other times, sadly, when there are no words to comfort a friend after the funeral. Whatever the occasion, food is meant to be enjoyed in the company of others.

In our home, when our daughters come to visit with their spouses and our sweet grandbabies, and after we've all been in the kitchen preparing a meal, laughing and talking all at once, it is our custom to sit down and pray before the meal. This is when my husband reminds us all, with his head bowed down in honor and praise, to "bless the hands of ALL those that prepared it." Yes, I have been blessed beyond measure.

Laurie Smith is a happily married wife, mother of two amazing daughters, Mimi to her grandbabies, Christian woman, and entrepreneur of the Etsy online shop, Willow Creek Sparrow, where she sells everything vintage along with her own handcrafted treasures. In her spare time, she enjoys picking up furniture off the curb, collecting old chairs, and perusing bookstores. Laurie is also a freelance photographer. One thing she loves most is a good pencil. Visit Laurie at www.etsy.com/shop/WillowCreekSparrow.

Mimi's Southern Banana Pudding

Ingredients:

- ¾ cup sugar
- 3 Tablespoons cornstarch
- Pinch of salt
- 2 cups of whole milk
- 1 cup of Half n Half OR cream (let me say right here, in a pinch use what you have on hand, I have used can milk, 1% milk, or any combo to get your 3 cups)
- 4 egg YOLKS mixed in bowl
- 1 TLB butter
- 2 tsp. vanilla (I also have used banana extract)
- 4-5 sliced bananas
- 1 box of vanilla wafers (use as many as you like)

Directions:

Mix sugar and corn starch.

Stir in 3 cups of your milk mixture.

Place on stove and stir the ENTIRE time so it doesn't burn or stick on you.

When it starts to thicken and bubble let it cook for 1-2 more minutes.

Remove from burner.

IMPORTANT STEP ~ tempering ~ so you don't have bits of cooked egg in your lovely creamy pudding, slowly add 2 cups of the hot pudding into the four egg YOLKS, stir and then with a small wire strainer, strain egg mixture back into your cook pot.

Place pot back on burner and bring to a soft boil (this won't take long) cook 1-2 minutes.

Remove from stove.

Add vanilla and butter.

Let pudding slightly cool (see my side note below).

Layering:

In your loveliest bowl layer your pudding on the bottom, then vanilla wafers, then bananas, ending with pudding. I like to sprinkle some vanilla wafers on the top, but that's up to you.

Side Note: about cooling before you layer.

My family loves this pudding when I make it right from the stove and I don't let it cool before layering. They like that the vanilla wafers soak up the hot pudding making the vanilla wafers soft. But if you use allot of bananas they tend to get a LITTLE mushy with that hot pudding. Experiment and see what your family loves! Enjoy!

Do not work for the food which perishes,
but for the food which endures to eternal life,
which the Son of Man will give to you,
for on Him the Father, God, has set His seal.

John 6:27 (NASB)

My Cinnamon-y Gooey Gluten-Free Adventure

Shawn Kay Sidwell

Taste and see that the Lord is good;
blessed is the one who takes refuge in Him.
Psalm 34:8 (NIV)

I love movies featuring writers. One of my favorites is *Stranger Than Fiction* starring Emma Thompson, Will Ferrell, and Maggie Gyllenhaal. For me, one of the best scenes is where Will's character (an IRS agent) brings Maggie's character (a nonconformist baker) a box of flours. She's more impressed with his thoughtfulness than she would have been by the traditional roses. Little did I know, a few short years later, I would be entrenched in the world of alternative flours.

I started cooking early. My mom used to quip that her children learned to cook out of self-defense. There's some truth to the statement. Because Mom hated the chore, my sister and I began fixing supper most nights while still quite young. We embraced finding recipes; chopping vegetables, sautéing, and watching meals take shape from a few simple ingredients. Baking became a natural segue. As a young mother and believer in homemade over store bought, I prepared most of our food, adding my own special touch to dependable recipes.

I suffered for years from a number of gastrointestinal distresses, not understanding what caused them. When I visited doctors, I came away with a diagnosis of Irritable Bowel Syndrome (IBS). But the diagnosis failed to satisfy me and never answered my most pressing concerns.

Then I learned about Celiac Disease. Celiac, a genetic autoimmune disorder which affects the villi of the small intestine, leaves sufferers unable to digest gluten, the protein found in wheat, rye, barley and a few lesser known grains. According to www.celiaccentral.org, "the body is attacking itself every time a person with celiac consumes gluten."

Though never tested for celiac, I opted to go gluten-free. My symptoms disappeared almost immediately. Over a year's period, I stayed mostly gluten free. When I broke protocol and couldn't resist a donut or chocolate chip cookie, the consequences were instantaneous and unpleasant.

About three years ago, I gave up gluten entirely. This meant a life of scrupulously reading labels and telling my friends and family I can't eat anything made with flour – a necessary nuisance, but most people understand.

As you probably guessed, processed gluten-free foodstuffs taste like cardboard, or worse, gritty and flavorless. Many of my attempts at home baked goods didn't fare much better. Like any form of culinary excellence, success came after abundant trial and error.

Once I decided to go gluten-free, I trotted off to the

library and checked out several cookbooks and tried a few recipes – some delicious, some not so much.

Then I branched out on my own. I crafted Ezekiel bread with gluten-free flour mix instead of the sprouted wheat. When I lugged it out of the bread machine it felt and looked somewhat like a lumpy brick and tasted much, much worse. Dry and crumbly, thick and bland, it was an experiment gone awry. I threw most of it away.

One Saturday last spring, on the return to Cheyenne from Fort Collins, my husband and I ran into a treacherous blizzard that lasted until we reached the Wyoming border. It took us almost two hours for what should have been a 45 minute trip.

Shaken and low on gas, we stopped at a convenience store just outside of town. I sat in the car shivering and staring at a giant poster enticing me to come inside and devour Cinnabon cinnamon rolls. Oh they sounded so good on that cold, snowy afternoon and I was half tempted to run in and grab a dozen, but I knew better.

By the time we got home, the cinnamon roll craving consumed me. I hopped on the Internet and typed in "gluten free cinnamon rolls." I found a Cinnabon copycat recipe, but didn't have all the ingredients. I made a few switches, and an hour or so later, I pulled warm, fragrant cinnamon rolls fresh from the oven.

They were almost as good as the real thing. I thought I had a keeper, but it turned out to be a fluke.

Gluten-free baking is tricky. Generally, you can't substitute flour for flour; it takes a combination of flours, starches and gums to create the proper structure for the dough to bind and the leavening to do its job.

I recently decided to bake cinnamon rolls again as a dessert for guests. Unable to find my handwritten note on the substitutions, I did my best to remember what I'd done originally. But the batter turned out runny. I made a last minute decision to convert them into cinnamon cupcakes. They tasted fine – everyone had seconds – but they weren't what I'd planned and I was disappointed.

My second attempt proved a bit better. Still, as I continued to add flour, the batter never achieved the proper consistency. The final product was okay, but came out more like cinnamon coffee cake than cinnamon rolls.

Challenged by the notion that the somewhat difficult task achieved perfection the first time and failed again and again afterwards, I was determined to get it right. On my third recreation, I did several things differently.

We live at 6,129 feet. High altitude baking requires adaption under normal circumstances. I decided to treat it as an elevation problem hoping it would do the trick. (The rest of my changes are explained in the recipe.)

Making the adjustments worked. I took the results to my grandchildren's house; everyone gobbled them up. Success! But just in case, I produced a final batch, with even more modifications.

As my husband bit into the concoction, he said, "Shawn, I think we have a winner!"

It's been an interesting journey. When shackled by my disorder, I had to regroup. Doing things as I've always done them no longer works, so every accomplishment feels like a triumph of the highest magnitude.

Still I feel blessed. God has supplied a way to provide my family with the goodies we've always enjoyed – and in the end the reward is sweet.

Shawn Kay Sidwell loves making people smile. She enjoys solving problems and taking care of clients at the business (DaybyDay Marketing) she runs with her husband, Andy. While she enjoys writing blog posts and composing eBooks, her true passion is fiction. In her spare time, she's busy penning short stories or working on one of her five (current) novels (with publishing credits in Standard and Woman's World.) Her greatest joy comes from spending time with loved ones. Shawn is happiest amongst a gathering of friends and family preparing ridiculously complicated and lavish meals and dessert items.

And all ate the same spiritual food;

1 Corinthians 10:3 (NASB)

Gluten-Free Cinnabon Recipe
Copycat Cinnamon Rolls

Dough:

- ½ cup milk*
- ½ tsp baking soda
- 1 T butter
- 1 ½ tsp xanthan gum*
- 1 packet (2 ¼ tsp) yeast
- 1 ½ tsp baking powder*
- ¼ cup granulated sugar
- ½ tsp salt
- ½ cup potato starch
- 1 large egg
- ¼ cup brown rice flour*
- ¼ cup oil (I used sunflower – the recipe called for olive)
- ¼ cup almond flour
- ½ tsp vanilla extract
- ¼ + 2 T cup sorghum flour*
- ¼ cup tapioca flour

Filling:

- 1/3 cup butter (softened)
- 2 T cinnamon
- ½ cup brown sugar

Frosting:

- 2 T butter (softened)
- ¾ C or more powdered sugar
- 3 T cream cheese (softened)
- ½ tsp vanilla extract

Directions:

In the bowl of a stand mixer, whisk together the yeast and sugar. Heat milk and 1 T butter in microwave to 110° - 115°F. Stir into yeast mixture and set aside to proof.

Meanwhile whisk together the potato starch, brown rice flour, almond flour, sorghum flour, tapioca flour, baking soda, xanthan gum, baking powder and salt.

Once the yeast is proofed, add in egg, oil and ½ tsp vanilla. Combine with mixer for a moment; then slowly add flour mixture. Turn your mixer up to medium-high and beat for 1½ minutes – beating the batter long enough is essential. Gluten-free flours are "thirsty." The dough will thicken and lose its stickiness as you beat it.

Cover a flat surface with a rectangle of plastic wrap (I used two sheets and joined them in the middle so they stuck together). Spread a thin layer of tapioca starch (use your hands to completely cover the entire area) across the surface. Place dough in center and pat it into a rectangle shape. Roll out to approximately a 13" x 10" rectangle; adding tapioca flour as necessary to keep it from sticking.

Spread softened butter over entire area of the dough.

Mix together the cinnamon and brown sugar and sprinkle evenly over the dough.

Roll up dough by starting on one of the shorter sides in order to form a log. Use the plastic wrap to help you "lift and roll" as you go along. Sprinkle with tapioca starch, as necessary.

Dip a sharp knife into the starch and cut into eight even pieces.

Place, cut side down, into a greased and floured pie plate or round cake pan (or use parchment paper). Cover with plastic wrap and a towel, place in a warm spot, and let rise for 15 minutes. Bake in 350°F oven for 22-27 minutes or until tops are golden brown.

Prepare icing by beating together softened butter and cream cheese and slowly adding powdered sugar until smooth. Stir in vanilla and a dash of salt. Drizzle over the tops of the rolls as soon as they come out of the oven. And enjoy!

*Notes: The original recipe called for 2/3 cup milk and 2 ½ tsp baking powder. The reduction both of these ingredients to the measurements listed above produced a dough rather than batter consistency. The original recipe also called for ½ cup brown rice flour. By exchanging half of it for sweet sorghum flour, I achieved softer, less gritty dough. I added the extra 2 T of flour because we live at high altitude. This might not be necessary at lower elevations. Some people have bad reactions to xanthan or guar gum, so I used a pinch of ground flax seeds, psyllium seed husk and chia seeds in two of my efforts, but returned to the use of xanthan gum when I actually had successful batches, so the results on this are inconclusive as to whether it makes a good substitution for this particular recipe. In my final two attempts, I also used the flat blade of the mixer rather than the dough hook and this may have also contributed to the final outcome.

Not Your Usual Quiche

Beth Lynn Clegg

I am the bread of life.
John 6:35 (NIV)

My paternal grandmother often made cucumber sandwiches for me as a special treat. This simple sandwich remains one of my favorites and was on the menu for a pre-nuptial party at my home over twenty years ago. This was not going to be just any old party. It was for my former stepdaughter. That's right. Former. Some might consider this an unusual occurrence, but Marilee and I enjoyed a special relationship that survived my divorce from her father. Although she'd urged me to keep things simple, an unknown force seemed to be pushing my limits of creativity.

Then there was her mother. To everyone's amazement, including ours, we became friends. Marilynne rivals Martha Stewart when it comes to presentation and execution of party details. It was going to be a challenge to prepare dishes that measured up to her expertise, but I said to myself, "Game on!"

Her father would also be attending. Okay, that pretty much identified the unknown force. There were probably unresolved issues simmering beneath the surface that inspired manifold reasons for wanting everything to be picture perfect. Days were spent searching through recipe files and cookbooks for tried and true selections that would enhance this memorable event. Two days before the party I arrived home from work and began do-ahead activities.

While 8 ounces of cream cheese softened to room temperature, I removed the crust from two loaves of bread, covered the loaves with damp cup towels like Grandmother had done, and set them aside. The crusts were placed on a cookie sheet, coated with olive oil and sprinkled with garlic powder, Italian spices, a dusting of parmesan, then cut into cubes and placed in a 200° oven for a couple of hours. The cooled croutons were placed in an airtight container.

As tantalizing smells filled the kitchen, a cucumber was pared and cut in pieces to fit a blender, along with ¼ cup grated white onion and other measured ingredients while juggling the phone between my shoulder and ear. A map with directions to my home was included in each invitation, but the winding residential streets and rolling hills in West Austin had people unfamiliar with the area concerned they'd get lost. To make matters worse, a one-way steep, curving driveway led up to my duplex with limited parking, but I assured everyone that complimentary valet service would be provided.

In the midst of these calls, cream cheese, cucumber, onion, ¼ cup of mayonnaise, 1 Tbs. lemon juice, ½ tsp. dill weed, salt and pepper to taste went in the blender. Shock waves rocked me when I removed the lid after twenty seconds and discovered cream of cucumber soup.

By focusing on getting guests to my home instead of what they might eat after arrival, I failed to drain the cucumber. Crucial mistake. What was I to do?

A 3 oz. package of cold cream cheese, more lemon juice, onion, and dill were dumped in the container. I prayed for a miracle as the machine whirred briefly. I eased the lid open. Smelled great. Tasted great. Now I had really *thick* cream of cucumber soup. There would be no miracle this night.

Why had I chosen to combine the cucumber with other ingredients? Why hadn't I made them as my grandmother had done? I knew from experience the sandwiches were delicious when well drained, wafer thin cucumber slices were placed on a cream cheese mixture spread over bread or toast points.

When my childhood brainwashing of waste not, want not, raised its ugly head, I resisted the urge to pour everything down the disposal. That decision made, I sealed the bread in plastic bags, cleaned the kitchen, took one last peek in the container, and fled the scene.

The following day, after sharing my nightmare experience, coworkers offered a wide variety of ideas, including down the disposal. When one opined I might turn the mess into a cheesecake, a solution hit me. After a quick stop at the grocery store, I returned home buoyed by a new can-do attitude, and set the oven temperature at 350 degrees before assembling new ingredients.

After lining two 9" pie plates and crimping the edges with store bought pie crust, (all culinary pride had vanished), I washed and drained two cans of baby shrimp, let four eggs come to room temperature, chopped a cup of cilantro, four green onions (green included), and a small diced Serrano pepper with seeds removed. The well beaten eggs and other fresh ingredients were added to the cucumber glop then poured over the shrimp that had been divided and sprinkled over the pie crusts. Forty-five minutes later my improbable concoctions were set out to cool.

To my amazement and delight, the quiche was delicious and I'd found a way to overcome adversity in the process. Who says miracles don't still happen? The party was filled with love and laughter, especially after the cucumber story made the rounds. Several wanted the recipe for what I dubbed, "grabbing victory from the jaws of defeat, or, how to transform cucumber spread into cucumber and shrimp quiche without really trying."

But if Marilee and her beloved, Haukur, took my experience and applied it to their marriage, what better gift could I have given them?

Beth Lynn Clegg, Houston, Texas, is an octogenarian who began her writing career after retiring from other endeavors. Her essays, fiction, nonfiction, poetry and prose have been published in anthologies, magazines, newspapers, poetry calendars and elsewhere. She treasures time spent with family and friends, volunteers at her church and Memorial Assistance Ministries, and also enjoys reading, cooking, gardening, and spoiling two cats.

Not Your Usual Quiche

Ingredients:

- 1 cucumber, pared and cut in pieces
- 3oz. and 8oz. packages of Cream Cheese
- ¼ Cup grated white onion
- 1/3 Cup mayonnaise
- 11/2 T lemon juice
- 1 T fresh dill or ½ t dry
- 1 Cup cilantro, chopped
- 4 spring onions, chopped, green included
- 1 small Serrano pepper, seeded and diced
- Salt and white pepper, to taste
- 4 eggs
- 2 cans baby shrimp, washed and drained
- 1 package 9" double pie crust
- 2 9" pie pans

Directions:

Line pie pans and crimp edges. Spread shrimp over bottom of crust. Set aside.

Let eggs and cream cheese come to room temperature. Set oven at 350 degrees.

Prepare cucumber, white onion, cilantro, serrano, spring onions and dill, if using fresh.

Place cucumber, cream cheese, mayonnaise, and lemon juice in blender. Pulse until incorporated. Add well beaten eggs. Adjust seasonings as needed and pour over shrimp lined pie pans.

Bake 45 minutes at 350 degrees or until knife comes clean after inserted in center.

In Memory of Grandma

Karey Christensen

And we know that God causes everything to work together
for the good of those who love God
and are called according to his purpose for them.
Romans 8:28 (NIV)

Hi Grandma. Today is October 8 and I thought it was about time for a letter. About me. And about how life has been without you. And I have so many questions. You left us, oh so very long ago.

When you drifted away, I was lost. I spent years trying to figure out why you left. I thought I had done something wrong, when all along, it was only because it was your time to go. Do you get to cook where you are now? Do you eat? I would send you one of our famous apple pies, if I could.

Does the air smell different there? Did you greet Dad when he came home? Were you there when he arrived? How did he look? Were his mother and father there? I'll bet he was happy to see them. Was he wearing his best blues uniform? I'll bet he looked handsome. I hope you hugged him. He always loved and respected you. He just didn't know how to tell you all those years after he lost touch and then you passed on. It was years later when he told me about it and you were long gone by then. I hope you were able to make up for lost time. Now he's up there with you, make sure you tell him I miss him wonderfully. I say wonderfully because, I know, one day in the very distant future, I'll see you'll all again.

Time without you has been like an old dried up apple pie. Where you want to eat that last piece sitting in the pie plate, the piece that is hard and crusty. I remember the first one I ever made without you. Oh what a specimen that was. You would have laughed at the results. We did. My daughter and I.

I've fallen over the years. And gotten back up again, many times, too many to count. Some days are harder than others. I won't lie, Grandma, it's been hard living without you. You are still my best friend. Do you hear me talk to you? I know one day we will all be together. I have learned this. I've learned some other things over the years, too. Mostly I've learned hard lessons. And my head is often filled with negative thoughts, but I'm looking for the right process through which to evolve so I can become the person you and I talked about me being, all those years ago.

Do you remember church, Pastor Randy, camp, and baking apple pie? I miss your apple pie. And hugs. And your humming when you cooked. And your stories. You'd talk for hours about life when you were a kid. Remember how we'd stand in the kitchen at camp and make apple pie? All that pealing, cutting, coring, sneaking bites, and finally baking the pies? I do. Still my favorite dessert. Then we'd go into the chapel and I'd listen to you play the organ while we'd eat the pie.

I miss you Grandma. Time without you has been hard. You passed on much too early, for me. I remember the day you passed, like it was just this morning. You had just met your first great-grandchild, my only child. As I laid her next to you on the bed to take pictures, you smiled a little. I know you smiled. The doctors said it was just a physical reaction and that you weren't really smiling. I knew they were wrong about that. I've got the pictures to prove it.

Anyway, I won't say goodbye, just see you later. I love you grandma. Give Dad a hug for me and tell him I miss him. Hug everyone and be sure to wait for me. While this letter to you might seem sad, and of course I'm crying, it's not meant to be sad.

I have a beautiful daughter. And I hope to teach her something you taught me, the message in 1 Corinthians 13:4-7 ESV, "Love is patient and kind; love does not envy or boast; it is not arrogant or rude. It does not insist on its own way; it is not irritable or resentful; it does not rejoice at wrongdoing, but rejoices with the truth. Love bears all things, believes all things, hopes all things, endures all things."

My love for you will endure, Grandma… until I see you and Dad again.

Karey Christensen, born and raised mostly in the Inland Northwest, has been an artist since conception. Taught to love drawing from her Grandmother. Taught to love good food and drink from her brother. Taught to love life and to laugh by her daughter. Taught to appreciate the love of a good man. Taught to love photography from her mom. And taught that forgiving, loving, and losing someone close to you, while making us miss them almost more than living, makes us who we are and appreciate living even more.

My Favorite Apple Pie

Pastry:

- 2 Cups All-Purpose Flour
- 1 Teaspoon Salt
- 2/3 Cup Plus 2 Tablespoons Shortening
- Note: We have also used about the same amount of butter, depending on your desired taste.
- 7 Tablespoons Cold Water

Filling:

- 1/3 to 1/2 Cup Sugar
- 1/4 Cup All-Purpose Flour
- 1/2 Teaspoon Ground Cinnamon
- 1/2 Teaspoon Ground Nutmeg
- 1/8 Teaspoon Salt
- 8 Cups thinly sliced peeled Tart Apples (8 medium)
- 2 Tablespoons Butter or Margarine - cold

Directions:

Into a medium sized bowl, mix the 2 cups flour and 1

teaspoon salt. Then, cut in shortening (or butter) using pastry blender (or pulling 2 table knives through the ingredients in opposite directions or even using just your hands to mix), until the mixture is about the size of small peas. Sprinkle in the cold water, about 1 tablespoon at a time, using a fork to toss the mixture until all flour is moistened and the pastry almost clings to the side of bowl (1 to 2 teaspoons more water can be added if necessary).

Gather the pastry you were working with into a ball, then divide in half. With each ball, shape them into 2 flattened rounds on a lightly floured surface. Take and wrap each round disc in plastic wrap and refrigerate for about 45 minutes or until dough is firm and cold, yet pliable and easy to form. This allows the shortening (or butter) to become slightly firm, which will help make the baked pastry more flaky. If, by chance you refrigerate the dough longer, let the pastry soften a bit before rolling it out.

Preheat oven to 425°F.

Take a floured rolling pin and roll one of the pastry rounds into a round disc that is about 2 inches larger than the upside-down 9-inch glass pie plate. Take the flattened out pastry and fold it into fourths and place it in the pie plate. Unfold the pastry shell and ease it into the plate, pressing it firmly against bottom and side.

In a large bowl, mix the sugar, the 1/4 cup flour, the cinnamon, nutmeg, and the 1/8 teaspoon salt. Stir in apples slowly, until they are well coated and mixed well.

Spoon the mixture into the pastry-lined pie plate. Cut the butter into small pieces and sprinkle it over the filling. Trim the overhanging edges of the pastry to 1/2 inch from rim of pie plate.

Roll the other round of pastry into approximately a 10-inch round. Fold the pastry into fourths. Unfold the top pastry over filling and cut slits so steam can escape, and trim the overhanging edge to about 1 inch from rim of plate. Fold and roll top edge under lower edge, pressing on rim to seal. Cover the edge of the pastry with a 2- to 3-inch strip of foil to prevent excessive browning.

Lastly, bake between 40 to 50 minutes or until the crust is brown and juices begins to bubble through slits in crust. Remove foil edging for the last 15 minutes of baking. Sit and enjoy a piece of warm pie with ice cream.

*It is like leaven, which a woman took
and hid in three pecks of flour
until it was all leavened.*

Luke 13:21 (NASB)

Shoofly Pie

Cindy Hansberry

So, whether you eat or drink, or whatever you do,
do all to the glory of God.
I Corinthians 10:31 (ESV)

Grammy loved to bake, cook, garden, and sew. She was delighted to share the fruits of her efforts as gifts to others. Grammy's Pennsylvania Dutch home was my favorite respite. While meat and potatoes were a staple of the Pennsylvania Dutch meals, schleck (Pennsylvania Dutch for sweets) was a requirement after every meal—yes, even breakfast.

When I stopped in to visit with her, we talked about family news while she made Shoofly pie—my favorite schleck.

Despite her heavily veined, arthritic hands, she pinched the freshly made pie shell edges into points. Then she added just the right amount of each ingredient to make her mother's Shoofly pie. Oh, how my mouth watered with anticipation to taste the crumb-topped cake layered on the gooey-bottomed pie.

While Grammy baked, she told me stories of her childhood days. Each Saturday, local farmers came to the Pottstown, Pennsylvania Farmer's Market to sell their chicken, beef, vegetables, and baked goods.

Starting Thursday morning through to Friday night, Grammy and her mother made Funny Cake, Shoofly, apple, and cherry pies. Early Saturday morning, they walked the three miles to market pushing a handmade wooden cart laden with the pies.

My great grandmother's pies were quite popular. Customers lined up in front of her market stall, and even spilled over into the space in front of the neighboring stalls. They wanted to be sure to have pie for Sunday dinner.

Interestingly, another pie purveyor, Amanda Smith, also sold her baked goods at the market. You may know the name—Mrs. Smith's Pies—from your grocery store experiences. Robert, Amanda's son, built the Farmer's Market business into the giant it is today.

As I watched Grammy's gnarled hands, my thoughts drifted back through my own childhood memories and stories my father shared. This kind woman sought opportunities to share her love with others. Her hands made dinner every Sunday for her family of 19. She never let anyone bring food or cook because these meals were her gifts to us.

Not wanting to muss her dress with stains as she baked, Grammy put on one of her handmade aprons. The aprons tied at her waist with the traditional pocket in its skirt. Grammy was a 5'4", medium-build lady who always pulled her gray hair into a bun in the back of her head. She donned the typical wire-rimmed granny glasses that fit snuggly over her ears. She wore stockings and laced shoes with wide heels. Her teeth were in her mouth at all times, except bedtime. Teeth in a glass on the bathroom sink always made me laugh, until I realized they might be mine one day.

Grammy's first-hand experience with the Great Depression shaped her into a frugal lady who knew that hard work was a necessity of life. Later, these disciplines benefited her greatly when a driver, who slid off a snowy road, killed her husband. She was left with three children between the ages of 10 and 14. My Grammy got a job at the local business school teaching typing on a manual typewriter. When she came home to her three children, she would begin her other jobs—mother, cook, baker, and seamstress.

While the children did their homework, Grammy's industrious hands made their clothes. Many times she disassembled her husband's old suits and used the fabric to make the children's clothes.

Suddenly, Grammy's sweet voice interrupted my thoughts, "Honey, will you put the schleck into the oven for me?"

"I sure will!" I eagerly replied.

Grammy's ever-busy hands demonstrated the love of Jesus—doing all for the glory of God.

As a recent empty nester, Cindy Hansberry is eager to apply the information she learned as a long-time member and officer of Little Rock American Christian Writers. With a belief that memories provide forever lessons to be embraced, she recently began a blog at www.yesterdaytoforever.wordpress.com. In addition to writing, she fulfills her passion for creativity by making greeting cards for family and friends. She and her husband live in Little Rock with their dog, Gracie.

Shoofly Pie

Ingredients:

- ¼ cup shortening
- 1 egg, slightly beaten
- 1 ½ cups flour
- ¾ cup hot water
- 1 cup brown sugar
- ¾ teaspoon baking soda
- 1 cup molasses or dark Karo syrup
- 10" pie crust

Directions:

Preheat oven to 400 F. Cut shortening, flour, and brown sugar into crumbs, and set aside. Dissolve baking soda in the hot water; add molasses and egg; mix well. Pour liquid mixture into pie crust. Top with crumb mixture.

Bake at 400 for 15 minutes; reduce temperature to 350 F and bake 30 minutes.

*"Also My bread which I gave you,
fine flour, oil and honey with which I fed you,
you would offer before them for a soothing aroma;
so it happened," declares the Lord GOD.*

Ezekiel 16:19 (NASB)

Going to Dallas

Jere Pfister

One generation shall commend your works to another,
and shall declare your mighty acts.
Psalm 145:4 (ESV)

In 1973 my husband and I moved from New Orleans, Louisiana to Okemos, Michigan. For us and our four young children it was an adventure we called, "Going to Dallas." Diagnosed with a genetic neurological disorder, our third child had become obsessed with the Dallas Cowboys. So every car trip, vacation, and adventure was forever referred to as, "Going to Dallas."

Two days after our move into our new home another family moved into a house two doors down. They had four sons the same ages as our daughter and three sons. They had a pool in their back yard while we had a large flat area for playing baseball. Their children did not know how to swim while my four were fish out of water and I had taken the Red Cross Lifeguard Training. Before the cold weather blew in I taught the four boys to swim and developed a close friendship with their mother.

Dorothy had grown up in Grand Rapids on the western

boarder of Michigan in a large Polish family. She was a baker and a good shopper who taught me how to save money and cook local foods. She took me to a local orchard that fall where they sold bushels of apples for a dollar. I have no idea what kind of apples just that they were for cooking. My only culinary skills were cake, brownies, and apple crisp. The only pie I made was lemon ice box pie with a vanilla wafer shell.

Determined that I could make a real pie crust she showed me several times to no avail. One day she agreed to watch all of the children while I tried my hand at making a pie crust on my own. I put all of the ingredients out on top of my portable dishwasher and began to make crusts. I must have destroyed eight crusts before resigning myself to failure.

Sometimes Dorothy and I took trips together, once to her mother's house in Grand Rapids. It was a cold fall day and we stopped at the sausage maker first and bought fresh Kielbasa for ourselves and her mother. We entered her mother's kitchen and it was like moving into another time zone.

This woman lived in her kitchen. It was light filled with large windows facing the backyard. The washing machine was in the kitchen. No dryer, the lines in the backyard dripped with a slow rainfall and next to the oven there were two wooden dryer racks with clothes and towels hanging. There were two bushels of apples on the floor and the table was covered with oil cloth. The scent of a spicy cake baking mixed with the smells and steam of the damp clothes. There were no counter tops; all preparation was done on the table and the top of the washer.

She sliced some of the sausages into small pieces and fried them in an old iron skillet. Then she scrambled six eggs for her youngest son who was in college. I don't remember him saying a word, just sitting at the table and shoveling in that delicious smelling platter of eggs and sausage. As soon as he dashed out of the room for classes she placed the pan cake that was in the oven on the table. It was perfect for a late cold rainy morning. And there we sat, in this beautiful kitchen with a woman who devoted her life to making sure her family was fed and mindful, forever long they lived, of the difference between prepared, boxed, frozen, or bakery food and scratch.

During the five years we lived in Michigan, I baked that same pan cake late at night so that the smells of baking would greet my children when the cold and snow seemed to permeate their bones and the dreariness of rainy, muddy spring days made all of us moody. And if I could make myself move fast enough the smell of apple cake would mingle with the smell of sausage or bacon on the stove top when they entered the kitchen. Those smells had become part of our lives in the cold of Michigan.

Dorothy and I had many adventures with our combined eight children, taking them on field trips and picnics, until her husband received a promotion which forced a move to Dearborn, Michigan near Detroit. I missed her but in the four years we were neighbors she had given me the skills to live in the Midwestern cold. She had even taught me to drive on icy roads after I slid my car into a large tree from braking too quickly. These driving lessons were for the sake of her children as much as mine since I had the only station wagon on the block and was the designated snow day driver for all the kids on Pawnee Trail.

Fast forward and our son Robby is now approaching fifty. And he's never lost his love for the Dallas Cowboys. In our last winter in Michigan, his resource teacher on a trip to Dallas during Christmas break met the Cowboys' star quarterback, Rodger Staubach. She told him about this student whose love for both Staubach and his team had helped him through many of his learning challenges. Rodger sent Rob an autographed photo and his autobiography. The photo hangs in Rob's home to this day, alongside his diploma from Texas Tech University. Little did we know when we accepted the transfer to Michigan that our little game would help produce such a good man and a mother who can still bake a cake.

Jere Pfister has been writing since the late 90's. She was a spiritual director at the Cenacle Retreat Center in Houston, TX from 1993 to 2000. She went back to school and earned a Masters of Arts in Theatre from the University of Houston in 2004. Married for fifty five years and still in Texas she and her husband Ted have four children and eight grandchildren who live in Austin, TX, Southern California, Lake Tahoe and Montana. And yes she still cooks.

Ode to Apple Cake

Ingredients:

- 4 Cups sliced apples
- ¾ Cups white sugar*
- 2 T flour
- 1 t cinnamon

Mix sugar, flour and cinnamon with apples and place in bottom of a two quart buttered casserole dish.

- ¾ cup flour
- ½ t salt
- ¼ t baking powder
- ¼ t soda
- 1 cup brown sugar*
- ¾ cup oats
- 1 cup brown sugar
- ½ cup butter melted

Directions:

Sift flour, salt, baking powder, and soda into bowl and add brown sugar and oats. Mix well and then add melted butter. Place on top of apples. Bake at 350 degrees for 45 minutes.

*Note: since last making this dish in the 1980's, I find the sugar content too strong and recommend decreasing both white and brown sugars by ¼ cup each.

The Best Carrot Cake They'd Ever Eaten

Linda Burklin

Give, and it will be given to you. A good measure, pressed down, shaken together and running over, will be poured into your lap. For with the measure you use, it will be measured to you.
Luke 6:38 (NIV)

"I'm getting married in October." My friend Elizabeth told me this often. "I don't know to whom, and I don't know what year, but I'm definitely getting married in October." We joked about this all the time. I would tell her that once she had the guy and the year figured out, I would make her wedding cake, since I once had a cake decorating business.

I was already married and had a young daughter, and I prayed Elizabeth would find a young man worthy of her. That summer, she returned from a six-month mission trip to Bolivia and she didn't seem herself. When I talked to her on the phone, my usually upbeat and cheerful friend was quiet and subdued. When I asked her why, she said she was just tired from traveling.

A couple of months later, I received a phone call from Elizabeth.

"Remember how I always said I'd get married in October?"

"Yes, of course."

"Well, I'm getting married in October! A month from now! And I want you to make the cake!"

I was dumbfounded. She had never mentioned dating anyone. Of course I had to hear the story.

During her time in Bolivia, she fell in love with a Bolivian man who was an assistant pastor at the church she attended. As a missionary, she was forbidden by the mission from having a relationship with a national, so she kept her feelings secret. When she left Bolivia to return to the USA, she thought she'd never see her Hugo again.

The church members in Bolivia, though, had noticed the blossoming romance and they approached Hugo about it after Elizabeth left. "What would it take to get you and Elizabeth together?" they asked.

"Well," he said, "I'd have to fly to the US to meet her family and ask her father's permission to marry her." Of course, he had no money and no hope of making the flight.

Hugo was so beloved by the congregation that they pooled their resources and bought him a plane ticket. Then they went the extra mile and collected enough money so that Hugo could buy an engagement ring for Elizabeth. The courtship and engagement would be very brief because Hugo's visa only allowed him to be in the country for a few weeks.

Now, the problem was that I had always said I'd make Elizabeth's wedding cake, but I could not afford a flight from Texas to South Carolina to be at her wedding.

"How much would you charge to make a wedding cake for 350 people?" she asked, ignoring my concerns.

"Oh, I wouldn't charge anything for *making* it," I told her. "I would just need help buying ingredients."

She spent a few minutes doing some research and then called me back. "Guess what? It's actually cheaper to fly you here to make the cake than it is to pay someone here to do it!"

In the days before my flight, I made dozens of royal icing roses and then carefully packed them in tins so they wouldn't be damaged in transit. Upon arrival in South Carolina, I would have one day to bake, one day to ice, and one day to decorate two large cakes. Elizabeth had also requested a groom's cake, and Hugo wanted it to be carrot.

I looked through my huge recipe collection but couldn't find a carrot cake recipe worthy of Elizabeth's wedding, so I created my own. In South Carolina, I baked two huge sheet cakes using my new recipe and then stacked and iced them with cream cheese frosting.

It was a huge hit--so many people told me it was the best carrot cake they'd ever eaten. The best thing for me was getting to spend time with my dear friend in the days before her wedding, and getting to meet her fiancé. Since that day in 1988, I've never made any other kind of carrot cake. I even have a gluten-free version now.

And Elizabeth and Hugo? Still happily married and serving the Lord in Bolivia.

Linda Burklin has been a storyteller and writer since childhood. Raised primarily in Africa, she wrote for and edited her college newspaper for two years while earning her English degree. Other than composing plays for her homeschool group, writing took a back seat during the years she was raising and home educating her seven children. For sixteen years, she has taught writing classes to her own and other homeschooled children, and authored the Story Quest creative writing curriculum. She has maintained a daily blog for ten years and has written a memoir and five novels. Her passion is speculative fiction. Please feel free to visit Linda at www.lindaburklin.com

Linda's Carrot Cake

Set oven at 350°

Ingredients:

- 4 eggs
- 2 cups all-purpose flour
- 1 ½ cups vegetable oil
- 2 teaspoons baking soda
- 2 cups sugar
- 1 teaspoon baking powder
- 1 teaspoon vanilla
- ½ teaspoon salt
- 2 teaspoons cinnamon
- 3 cups grated carrots
- 1½ cup chopped walnuts

Directions:

In a mixing bowl, beat the eggs. Add the oil, sugar and vanilla and beat again.

Sift together the flour, soda, baking powder, cinnamon and salt. Add slowly to the egg mixture, beating on low speed.

When the dry ingredients have been thoroughly incorporated, stir in the carrots and walnuts by hand until everything is well-mixed.

Pour into a greased and floured 9x13 pan. Bake at 350°
for 40-50 minutes or until a toothpick comes out clean.
Cool completely before icing.

Linda's Cream Cheese Icing

Soften ½ cup butter and 8 oz. cream cheese, then beat
together until mixture is very smooth and lump-free.
Beat in 1 teaspoon of vanilla.

Add powdered sugar until you have a nice spreadable
consistency—it should take about a pound. Spread on
cake and then store cake in fridge. The icing will get
very firm in the fridge.

From Home and Heart

Janis Bell

"For I know the plans I have for you"
declares the Lord, "plans to prosper you and not to harm you,
plans to give you hope and a future."
Jeremiah 29:11 (NIV)

A lot of people like bread pudding – not me – I won't eat it.

I know it's an international favorite. It's a popular dessert in Britain, Puerto Rico, Mexico, France and Argentina. Louisiana Creoles and other Southerners have made it a mainstay of American cuisine.

No matter what sauce – whiskey, rum, caramel, vanilla or lemon – I can't be enticed. I'm not a picky eater either.

My eighth-grade homeroom teacher, Mrs. Clark, was responsible for my aversion. She asked me to make a batch of bread pudding to take to her friend who was sick and needed cheering.

You see Mrs. Clark had taken me on as her special project that year. I was a transfer student from parochial school and Mrs. Clark took me under her wing to help me adjust to the mysterious and frightening ways of public school education.

Things went well until Mrs. Clark received my transcript from St. Michaels and she determined I was a slacker and lazy and working way short of my potential. She quoted test scores and teacher evaluations as evidence of my hopeless state.

She said the problem was that I just hadn't been stimulated enough.

"You daydream and mope around because you don't have enough to keep you busy. I'll fix that," she exclaimed.

So every morning in homeroom, Mrs. Clark would hand me a list of extra jobs to do for her in school, plus after-school projects for me to do at home when I'd finished my schoolwork.

Mrs. Clark was a Home Economics teacher, so most of my extracurricular tasks involved cooking or sewing – skills that were new to me.

I balked at her prodding and constant lectures at first, but eventually grew to like the attention and started to thrive. By the time the bread pudding project surfaced, I was a content teacher's pet.

Mrs. Clark gave me her favorite bread pudding recipe. She was very thorough with her instructions, and assured me that bread pudding was the easiest dessert ever to make. It was her sick friend's favorite, and she looked forward to surprising her friend Friday after school.

My bread pudding looked perfect– just like the picture from the magazine. I made it late Thursday night and cradled it carefully on the school bus ride Friday morning.

It really smelled good, too. I had to fight off the boys on the bus who wanted to take a taste. But it arrived safely and Mrs. Clark was very pleased.

That was the first of dozens of bread puddings I made for Mrs. Clark, my family, and friends over the years. And that is why I don't eat it – I had made so many and eaten it too much.

Mrs. Clark gave me many other recipes and cooking techniques, but I'll never forget this first attempt, which taught me the warmth of giving food from home and heart, and the joy it brought to me in return.

This loving and devoted teacher taught me responsibility and the art of making good food for comfort and fellowship.

Janis Bell admires the simple things in nature and life. This attitude has influenced her style of writing, art, and photography. She's drawn to the straightforward and uncomplicated world and its treasures. Janis graduated from The University of Texas at Austin. After a career as a commercial interior designer, she has pursued writing and art projects in two contrasting settings of a big city and a small mountain town. She lives in Houston, Texas, and Georgetown, Colorado, with her husband, Richard. Please contact Janis at janbell@utexas.edu.

Mrs. Clark's Old-Fashioned Bread Pudding

Prep: 15 min.
Total Time: 60 min.
Serves: 8

Ingredients:

- 2 cups milk
- 1/4-cup butter or margarine
- 2 eggs, slightly beaten
- 1/2-cup sugar
- 1 teaspoon ground cinnamon or nutmeg
- 1/4-teaspoon salt
- 6 cups soft bread cubes (about 6 slices of bread)
- 1/2-cup raisins
- Whipping (heavy) cream

Directions:

Heat oven to 350°F. In 2-quart saucepan, heat milk and butter over medium heat until butter is melted and milk is hot.

In large bowl, mix eggs, sugar, cinnamon and salt. Stir in bread cubes and raisins. Stir in milk mixture. Pour into ungreased deep round pan.

Bake uncovered 40 to 45 minutes or until knife inserted 1 inch from edge comes out clean. Serve warm with whipping cream.

The Baker

Brenda Fiola

He told them another parable: "The kingdom of heaven is like yeast that a woman took and mixed with three measures of flour until all the dough had risen."
Matthew 13:33 (NET)

Chocolate is the answer. Who cares what the question is.
Unknown

To say I have a sweet tooth is a major understatement. Ever since I was a little girl, my favorite smell in all the land was of a bagful of Halloween candy. In fact, my sweet tooth is probably to blame for the reason my mother always calls me a "baker". It wasn't because I had a desire to be creative or experiment with my culinary skills in the kitchen. It was because I wanted something sweet to eat and I couldn't find it in the house!

One Saturday, when I was about 13 years old, I needed something sweet to eat, so I scavenged through the cupboards and pantry to see what ingredients I could find. Aside from butter, flour, and some powdered sugar, I wasn't striking much luck. I rummaged through my mother's cookbooks to see what I could possibly make with just these three simple ingredients. After a while, I found it – Sandies! Right away, I mixed the dough, formed them into rounded balls, baked them, and rolled them in the powdered sugar. Voila! I had cookies!

I didn't really think much about them at first, but my mother raved about how beautiful they were. She claimed that no one could just open up a cookbook, choose a recipe, and make it come out exactly the way it looked in the picture. I looked at them and agreed they were kind of pretty, but mostly I was just happy to satisfy my sweet tooth. And, in actuality, I really would have preferred something chocolate.

For the next few years, I continued to bake cookies and desserts as dictated by my sweet tooth; mostly simple recipes such as Toll House Cookies, banana bread, a couple of frozen pies – any recipe that worked with whatever ingredients my mother had in the house. I do remember one time when I was a little adventurous and thought I would make some taffy. I smashed up some marshmallows, mixed in a little peppermint extract, wrapped them in wax paper, and put them in the freezer to thicken. As I recall, my dad was the lucky one to get the first sample of my delicious taffy after dinner, and I distinctly remember him saying, "Hmm, it tastes like toothpaste."

As I grew older and became a driver, I realized I could actually drive to the store and purchase already-made sweets for my tooth, rather than making them. So I took some time off from being "the baker". In fact, it wasn't until after I had two children of my own that I began baking again. And this time, the exciting thing about it was that I could decide what I wanted to make FIRST, and THEN get all of the ingredients I needed, including a regular supply of chocolate!

I have never considered myself to be a good cook, let alone a good baker, but my mother hasn't given up on me. To this day, when my husband makes a sarcastic remark about my cooking, my mother still says those magic words, "Well, that's because she's a baker!" (And for some reason, he thinks this is funny.)

So, whether you're a baker (or not), here is a recipe that is guaranteed to knock your socks off. It has been a family favorite of ours for many years, and I receive nothing but compliments every time I bake it. And if you happen to be a chocolate lover like me (and now my daughter), your sweet tooth is in for a big treat!

Brenda Fiola lives in California with her husband, Rich, and has three adult step-sons, and a teen-aged son and daughter. When not satisfying her sweet tooth, she enjoys hiking with her dog, going to the beach, and spending time with friends. Brenda has spent the last nine years working in the public education system with elementary school children and is known by her family and friends for writing the cleverest Christmas letters of all time.

The house of Israel named it manna,
and it was like coriander seed, white,
and its taste was like wafers with honey.

Exodus 16:31 (NASB)

Knock Your Socks Off Carmelitas

Ingredients:

- 32 caramel squares, unwrapped
- ½ cup heavy cream
- ¾ cup butter, melted
- ¾ cup brown sugar, packed
- 1 cup flour
- 1 cup rolled oats
- 1 teaspoon baking soda
- 6 ounces semisweet chocolate chips

Instructions:

Preheat oven to 350. Grease an 8x8 pan or you can line with aluminum foil or parchment paper for easier removal. The caramel can get sticky. (Can also be made in a 9x13, just double the ingredients.)

In a mixing bowl, combine melted butter and brown sugar. Add flour, oats, and baking soda. Mix until combined.

Divide the cookie mixture in half and pat half of the mix into the bottom of the 8x8 pan. Bake for 10 minutes and remove.

While baking, combine the caramels and heavy cream and stir until completely smooth. Can also be melted in the microwave, just stir after every 30 seconds being careful not to let it burn.

Remove pan from the oven and sprinkle chocolate chips over the crust. Pour caramel mixture over the chocolate chips and crumble remaining cookie dough on top.

Return to oven and bake for 15-20 minutes until the edges are lightly brown.

Once removed from oven allow them to completely cool so the caramel can set up. The caramel is like molten caramel right out of the oven and you want to let it cool. You can speed up the cooling process by putting it in the fridge if needed.

Finney-Coe Hot Fudge Sauce

Leslie Fink

I shall not die, but live and declare the works of the Lord.
Psalm 118:17 (KJV)

I was born in Ypsilanti, Michigan and had a very large extended family. My mother had six siblings, three brothers and three sisters, and I have fourteen cousins. We grew up very close together and we all spent a lot of time at my grandparent's big house on Farmer Street. My grandmother loved to cook and since my grandfather had a major sweet tooth there were always sweets in her home. In our family's opinion her sweets and baking were by far the best in Washtenaw County.

My grandmother had a small kitchen with a very large, fancy dining room. The dining room was for special occasions and I never felt quite comfortable sitting there. All of my fondest memories are sitting at her tiny Formica table in that small kitchen, just waiting for her culinary magic to begin. My grandmother made everything better than I could get anywhere else. From something as simple as toast with real butter, which I never had at my home, to her famous hot fudge sauce, a recipe we've been able to trace through five generations to my Great-Grandmother Finney.

When my sister and I sat at that table waiting for her

very special hot fudge sauce, Grandma told us stories of how she grew up, how she met Grandpa, and about Mom. We loved hearing these stories and begged her to tell them to us over and over as she cooked the hot fudge sauce. I think that hot fudge sauce actually takes about ten minutes to make, but somehow she managed to turn those 10 minutes into an hour of Coe family story entertainment. I'm not sure what she was doing at the stove that whole time, but as children, we really didn't care. We just wanted the stories and the hot fudge sauce.

Sometimes, we would walk in Grandma's kitchen and say, "I'm thirsty." She would always answer, "I'm Friday, let's go out Saturday and have a Sundae." That in itself got me in the mood for a sundae with her hot fudge sauce, and I would immediately start begging for one. She, of course, acted like it was this huge imposition, but she would put on her kitchen apron and start the stove and the conversation. Now that I am a parent myself, I can see that the making of the hot fudge sauce was an opportunity for my grandmother to ask us questions about our day and get us to share with her and talk about things that we probably never would have. I now see she had a wonderful and loving ulterior motive.

One of the best secrets of Grandma's hot fudge sauce was what happened to it overnight. Whatever we didn't eat, Grandma would put in the fridge in a bowl. She always told us we could warm it up for the next day – but it never made it because during the night, my sister and I would sneak down stairs and get spoonfuls of this wonderful chocolate concoction and eat it cold out of the fridge. It was even more amazing that way than it was on ice cream. We rarely crossed paths in the night, but if we did, we pretended we were going to the bathroom or getting a drink of water. The next morning the hot fudge sauce was always gone and Grandma never spoke a word of it. Obviously she knew what we were doing at night, but she pretended not to.

This wonderful tradition of hot fudge sauce has continued at our own home as well and when we moved from Michigan to Texas, and my grandma was no longer living near us to make it, my mom carried on her tradition. We even continued the tradition of eating the hot fudge sauce by the spoonful during the night.

Once I became a parent and my kids got older I continued the tradition and made hot fudge sauce for them. It was always a favorite treat of theirs growing up. My son, Hunter, called it "the secret recipe." He even asked me if one day when he got married I would give him the secret recipe to the hot fudge sauce so he could make it for his kids. Our hot fudge sauce is one of the things my daughter Haley misses most in college. I am patiently waiting for my children to have their own children to bring into my kitchen so I can make them the hot fudge sauce. I will share stories with my grandchildren of their mother and father growing up and continue the tradition that my amazing grandmother gave me.

Leslie Fink lives in Houston, Texas with her husband, Richard, and their two children, Hunter and Haley. She grew up in Huntsville, Texas and moved to Houston in 1988. She has been a paralegal since that time and enjoys her career. She loves spending time with her family, listening to live music, spending time with her miniature dachshund, Coco Puff, and traveling whenever possible.

Finney-Coe Hot Fudge

Ingredients:

- 1 Cup Sugar
- 1/4 Cup Cocoa
- 1/4 Cup Margarine
- 1/4 Cup Whole Milk
- 2 Teaspoons Vanilla
- 1 Tablespoon Karo Syrup

Directions:

Cook all but Vanilla to a boil. Boil 1 minute. Add Vanilla, remove from heat, cool. Serve over ice cream.

Any leftovers pour into a bowl and refrigerate overnight. Watch and see how much is left in the morning.

How sweet are Your words to my taste!
Yes, sweeter than honey to my mouth!

Psalm 119:103

The Ends Have All The Vitamins

Terri Lacher

Day by day, continuing with one mind in the temple,
and breaking bread from house to house,
they were taking their meals together
with gladness and sincerity of heart.
Acts 2:46

Growing up in the 1950's in a small community in southern California, my siblings and I learned very early on the meaning of sharing what we had with others. Our parents grew up during the Depression and moved from the Arkansas Ozarks to relocate in California. Bringing their rich traditions with them, they settled down and made new friends through church gatherings, and our family grew to include multiple cousins for me and my brother to play with.

The core of our gatherings were centered around three things:

- Someone always brought out a banjo or guitar, and the music was lively as they sang their favorite mountain ballads.

- The men sat on the outskirts, drinking strong coffee from their saucers and "shooting the breeze" as my father used to call it.

- There were the assortment of the pies, cakes, and homemade breads spread out on the table for us kids to run by and snatch a piece of when no one was looking.

That third thing was the highlight, with a greater selection of baked goodies during the holidays for us to sneak. We crammed butter and sugar sandwiches into our mouths as we ran around willy-nilly in the late afternoons.

By today's standards, we would have been considered poor, but we never knew it. If a family came through our town in the winter months and their car broke down, our father invited them to come home and share a meal with us, telling our mother to set out a second loaf of bread and put more water in the beans. We squeezed in around our table, extensions in, chairs and stools brought in, including Mom's sewing chair, and shared our meal with complete strangers. Mom would cut the first slices of the freshly made bread as the wonderfully yeasty aroma filled our crowded kitchen, all of us reaching with outstretched hands for that first slice. I usually got the end of the bread, and so I wouldn't feel bad about it, Dad said the end was where all the vitamins were, which left the nicely sliced middle pieces for the company. It was a wonderful time in our family. We had a roof over our head, indoor plumbing, new friends, and each other. And we had homemade bread.

As the years past, our families grew up and we all moved off to different places. Our grandparents, aunts and uncles, and then our parents passed away as well, leaving my brother and our younger sister and me with a heart full of love and good family memories. My brother's wife learned to make her version of the homemade bread, and my sister stayed with the traditional white loaves, which I still count on when we get together for Thanksgiving or Christmas. I was the rebel child, I guess, and decided my children needed to eat healthy. I searched around and found a honey whole-wheat version. It wasn't long until it became a favorite around our house, but because of work schedules, it seemed the only time we really got to enjoy it with the rest of our family was around the holiday season.

When my children were small, they required many activities to keep them busy, and even more supervision to keep them out of trouble. Bread-making became a routine experience, as I enlisted the assistance of my smaller boys to keep them from fussing with the older ones. More often than not, it was our youngest son whose three-year-old fingers were just the right size to work the dough. He balanced on a kitchen chair, bent over the bread board on the table, and watched and copied the movements for kneading the dough. We set the timer for ten minutes to keep him from asking a hundred times if his bread was ready yet. The yeast always rose, and the bread was always nearly perfect, and we had time together that we would miss dearly years later in our lives.

We discovered new additions to the bread dough to make it more interesting. After the first rise, we rolled out the dough and poured in melted butter and cinnamon sugar before rolling it up into loaves. On another occasion, I discovered that freshly ground trail mix added to the butter mixture made a wonderfully delicious breakfast bread. It was a great way to sneak healthy ingredients into the kids' fast-food diets. When their lives were filled with busy school schedules, and I returned to work, it was a rare treat to have time to make a couple of fresh loaves of bread for our weekend meal. It was a sure guarantee that the kids would find time to come home and eat if they knew a fresh loaf of honey wheat bread was waiting for them on the table.

Now our own kids are grown and scattered with their families across the country. Nothing pleases me more, though, than when they come home for the holidays and inquire if, just by chance, there might be some home-made bread. When my sister and her family are able to be part of the celebration, I know I can expect her to bring her loaf of white bread. As we sit together as a family, extensions in the table, chairs brought from around the house, including the sewing room chair, it brings all those good memories from our childhood together. I smile at these thoughts, especially after one of us passes the plate of fresh sliced bread around. It takes me back to a time when our father sat at the head of the table, and Mom handed out the slices of hot bread. I find myself reaching for my favorite end piece, because, after all, "the ends have all the vitamins."

Terri Lacher, author and speaker, presents her views on life with humor and enthusiasm. Her passion for writing began in early childhood, sitting in a library with her grandmother, the local librarian, surrounded by books. Her writing can be found in Chicken Soup For the Soul books, and in an online Texas history magazine. Her newspaper column called, "Cobwebs In the Attic," is filled with heaping tablespoons of humor "to help life's difficulties go down easier." Terri and Bob share a blended family of six grown kids, twelve grandchildren, and Samson, a goofy Labrador. Please feel free to contact Terri at btlacher@sbcglobal.net.

*He distributed to everyone of Israel,
both man and woman,
to everyone a loaf of bread and a portion of meat
and a raisin cake.*

1 Chronicles 16:3 (NASB)

Terri's Honey Wheat Bread

(From the Scott-Gilbert Family Cookbook, 1990)

Ingredients:

- 2 pk. dry yeast
- ½ cup warm water
- ¼ cup Butter Flavored Crisco
- 3 cups of whole wheat flour
- 1/3 cup honey (I try to use local honey if possible)
- 1 tsp salt
- 1 ¾ cups warm water
- 3-4 cups unbleached flour (depending upon how much wheat flour used. You may add 1 more cup of wheat flour, reducing the amount of unbleached used by the same amount)

Directions:

In large mixing bowl, dissolve yeast in ½ cup of warm water. Add next six ingredients. Blend together until well mixed. Gradually add 3 cups of unbleached flour, stirring until mixture forms a large ball. Turn onto floured board, knead in the remaining cup of flour. Knead further (approx. 10 minutes) until smooth and elastic in appearance. Place in greased bowl, cover, let rise until double in size (approx. 1 – 1½ hours). Punch down, divide in half and roll out to rectangle approx. 8 x 15 inches. Roll up each rectangle (jelly roll style) and place in greased loaf pans, letting dough rise again until nearly 1½ times its size. Bake in preheated oven at 375 degrees until done, about 35 minutes. I usually butter the exposed tops after the bread has baked for about 20 minutes and return it to the oven until done.

Sometimes for something different, when I roll out the dough before putting it in the loaf pans, I have added melted butter with sugar and cinnamon. For a heartier bread, I have also added trail mix (slightly ground in the food processor) to the cinnamon and butter and then roll it into the loaf pans. It makes a really healthy and delicious breakfast bread!

*Kneading the dough is an excellent activity for pre-schoolers. Their little fingers have just the right touch to not overwork the dough, and spend time with Mom or Grandma.

Bon Appetit!

Our Crumbling Experience

Hannah Williams

And the house of Israel call its name Manna, and it is as
coriander seed, white; and its taste is as a cake with honey.
Exodus 16:31 (YLT)

A party without a cake is just a meeting.
Julia Child

It was my mom's birthday and I decided to bake one of
her most favorite cakes. One she does not eat often. A
raspberry vanilla cake.

I am not a raspberry person myself but I knew she
would love it. The thing was, I made it last minute.
Looking back I realize this was not the smartest idea, but
I did buy the ingredients the night before, so that counts
for something. Right?

At the time, I was lifeguarding for our city's local pool,
which I had to open that day. But that wouldn't be a
problem. I had planned it all out and made sure I had
enough time to mix, bake, and ice the cake all before I
had to go to work.

In theory, all that planning sounded good. But I had
forgotten about the extra time needed to let the cake
cool BEFORE I added the raspberry filling and icing.

The other mistake I made was not cutting the bottom layer flat (or better yet, spooning out some of the cake middle to create a shallow dip) so that the filling would not spill out over the sides. So there I was putting hot, yes hot, raspberry filling on the bottom cake layer that was rounded from rising, all while trying to get my husband's fingers out of the icing and raspberry bowl.

I didn't realize that would be a problem so I iced the entire cake in vanilla, and topped it off with gorgeous fresh raspberries. Oh I was so proud, and as I stood in the kitchen beaming at my prized cake and boasting in the triumph of what I expected to be delicious, I began to watch the cake fall apart, crumbling and melting onto the plate as the clock sounded a reminder that it was time to leave for work.

With no time to put on clothes over my swimsuit, my husband drove me to mom's house while I held the cake (looking much like a volcano experiment for an elementary science fair) gently in my lap.

The record highs that week (with temperatures over 100° in Texas) and much too many speed bumps were not helping my cake crisis. And the screaming ensued. I screamed for my husband to take the speed bumps more slowly. I screamed about the cake melting from the heat. And I screamed about being late for work as I frantically tried to "smush" back together the icing and raspberry that oozed from what resembled earthquake cracks in the cake. I had the remnants all over my fingers.

My poor husband looked at me like I was crazy, but he's

a trooper so in military fashion he put on his game face, determined to get us to my mom's house - before the cake melted completely, before I was late for work, and before I crumbled along with my cake.

Finally, we arrived at mom's house and I jumped out of the car, ran across the lawn in my life-guard suit, cake in hand, and headed for the front door. Raspberry filling oozed out everywhere!

Thankfully, she was expecting us and ran out the door to meet me halfway. Grateful to place the cake in her hands, I ran back to the car so my husband could drop me off at work.

Mom texted me later that day with the rest of the story. She had placed various cooking utensils in the cake, hoping to mold it back together before putting it in the fridge. But when she went back to the fridge later to see the progress, she only saw half the cake on the plate. Finally, after looking all over the kitchen, she discovered the other half of the cake stuck to the inside of the fridge door and all over the condiment bottles.

I busted out laughing at her text and perfect description of what I call an 'I love Lucy' moment and that became the year known for our crumbling experience. We gathered around at her house later that day and ate the crumbling cake, propped up with toothpicks, chopsticks, and shish kabob sticks to hold it together. It looked like a one year old had gotten her hands on it, and still it was the most yummy and special cake mom said she'd ever had.

Hannah Williams is a native Texan who grew up in Farmers Branch. She loves spending time with her family and laughing about all the 'Lucy' mishaps she and her mom and sister get into. She graduated from Texas Woman's University in Denton with a Bachelor's in Kinesiology and Minor in Education where she was certified as a Coach and Physical Education teacher K-12. After moving to Georgia when her husband, Bo, was re-stationed for military orders, she got her first teaching and coaching job. But she turned in her whistle to become a mom (her true dream job) to her beautiful daughter, Abigail.

Raspberry "Crumble" Cake

Cake Recipe:

- Use your favorite vanilla cake recipe or pick a box up at your local grocery store ☺
- Use 2 small round cake pans

Raspberry Cake Filling

Ingredients:

- 1½ cup frozen raspberries
- 1 TBSP cornstarch
- 2 TBSP lemon juice
- ¼ cup sugar

Put all ingredients into a saucepan. Bring mixture to boil. Stir until thick. Cool.

Easy Vanilla Buttercream Frosting

Ingredients:
- ½ cup butter (softened)
- 4½ cup powdered sugar

- 1½ tsp vanilla extract
- 5-6 TBSP 2% milk

Beat in softened butter until light and fluffy. Beat in powdered sugar, vanilla, and milk.

Cake Assembling Directions

Bake cake and let cool. Cut middle layer flat (or with slight dip).

Cook raspberry filling and let it cool.

When all is cool, spread raspberry filling on bottom layer cake.

Ice entire cake.

Add fresh raspberries as garnish on top.

Makes one 2-layer round cake.

Gammy's Secret Ingredient

Peggy Redelfs

He brought me to the banqueting house,
and his banner over me was love.
Song of Solomon 2:4 (ESV)

When my dad was young, maybe 11 or 12, he and his friends were playing with fire crackers when those in his pocket caught fire. His one leg was so badly burned that the doctor wanted to amputate it.

Gammy told the doctor, "If you do, I will kill you!"

The doctor took Gammy's threat seriously and my dad's leg healed. Even though he suffered severe scaring, my dad's walking was never affected. In fact, he later served as a drill sergeant in World War I.

Gammy was my paternal grandmother and her passion for her children was evident in her every action, although her strength and intelligence were disguised by her tiny stature, flowered house dresses, and barely grey hair pulled back into a bun.

Widowed in her early 30's, she raised five children and times were tough. My dad recalls the joy of getting an orange at Christmas. My father and his three sisters and brother grew up close and they frequently gathered at her house on Sunday afternoons where she served her sauerbraten, potato pancakes, and stolen. Her small home overflowed with her family.

Gammy's passion for her children could be tasted in her passion for cooking. And, she rarely used recipes. I watched her make her stolen and just took notes. She did not measure much and would put a spice on the tip of a knife. I do have her recipes for her chocolate cookies and her sugar cookies. When the family would drop by she always had a big, galvanized, speckled, blue pot of coffee on the stove. I loved to watch her make coffee. She would fill the pot with water, dump in the coffee, and just before it had completely brewed, she would break an egg, toss it in, shell and all. She said the egg clarified the coffee. Her coffee was better than Starbucks.

Gammy cooked everything! My dad was a hunter and would bring back wild game, which she would cook. Rabbits might end up in a sauerbraten. Fish would be poached in a tomato, onion, and green pepper sauce. She made pork chops that melted in your mouth. For herself - she loved limburger cheese and onion sandwiches on rye bread.

In Gammy's later years my father checked on her daily, dropping by after work. She still baked, although not as often. Sometimes after visiting his mother, he would come home with her "crullers," lovely twisted doughnuts. They were my favorite – warm, crispy, twisted doughnuts, unlike anything Dunkin puts out. I do think love is the added ingredient that made her cooking so good. When I think of Gammy, I think of her crullers.

But it was her stolen I loved so much, a most delicious coffee cake. To this day, I bake Gammy's stolen every Christmas to give as gifts to my best friends, which is no small task. The first day is spent soaking raisins in whiskey to plump up and flavor them. Mixing is usually done the second day, in the evening, so the dough can rise over night in the oven. On the third day, I shape the loaves and let them rise before baking them. The dough is very heavy so it does not rise very much, not like usual breads. I then wrap the cake in foil and tie with red plaid ribbon, leaving them in the oval foil pans they are baked in. I also bake it for myself from time to time and greedily eat one, while freezing the others.

Gammy's cooking was the best. I thought so as a little girl, and I think so now as an adult. And, as I reminisce over her passion for her family, which she demonstrated in her cooking, I believe I've discovered her secret ingredient… one well rounded cup of love.

Peggy Redelfs is an 88 year old senior (although she feels more like a freshman) who has three children, 4 grandchildren, and two cats. Upon graduating from Washington University, she worked as a dress designer, then married and moved to Pennsylvania where she raised her children. Returning to St. Louis, she became a real estate broker until she bought a "winter home" in New Orleans. Losing it to Katrina, she now lives in Missouri where she gardens, makes her own greeting cards, and illustrates her daughter's (Dr. Anne Redelfs) books, The Awakening Storm and Evading the Storm. Please feel free to contact Peggy at peggilegg@hotmail.com

Gammy's German Stollen

Have ingredients at room temperature:

First day:

- Soak 1/2 package of white raisins
- 1/2 package of brown raisins
- 4 ounces of chopped citron
- 4 ounces of slivered almonds in 1/2 cup of whiskey; I use Jim Beam

Second day: I usually do this in the evening, cream well:

- 1 stick fairly soft butter
- 1/2 cup oil
- 1 1/2 cup sugar, then add 2 eggs, 1 grated lemon rind

MIX, then add 2 packages of dry yeast (check date) mixed in 1 cup warm milk with 1 tablespoon sugar until it has become spongy and frothy. Mix well, then add 4 to 5 cups of flour (use bread flour NOT pastry flour). Use beater until stiff then mix by hand. Then add raisin mixture and KNEAD. Place in large bowl, cover with saran and put in a lukewarm oven overnight. I keep the oven light on but no real heat.

Third day: Mixture should have risen but not a whole lot. Shape into loaves (I use the small oval aluminum pans). Make 4 or 5 loaves. LET RISE!!!!!! Usually about 2 to 3 hours. Put into 400 degree oven BUT turndown to 350 degrees. Bake 40 to 45 minutes. Check with tooth pick. WATCH!!!! Cover with foil it they get too brown. When done, cool and top with powdered sugar, and then wrap for Christmas gifts.

Reindeer Run

Tasha Wilks

And, lo, the angel of the Lord came upon them, and the glory of the Lord shone round about them: and they were sore afraid. And the angel said unto then, Fear not: for, behold, I bring you good tidings of great joy, which shall be to all people. For unto you is born this day in the city of David a Savior, which is Christ the Lord.
Luke 2: 9-11 (KJV)

Christmas is undoubtedly my favorite time of year. As soon as the leaves start changing colors, I press play to watch the classic 1950's "White Christmas," sip on a cup of hot apple cider, and start unpacking my (almost) overwhelming tubs of winter decorations. My goal is to sprinkle Christmas joy in every room of my home.

Like many of you, our family has traditions that are added each year because of what interests or inspires our kids at the time. Last year, instead of doing naughty things, our Elf of the Shelf was caught doing kind gestures. When our kids followed suit with each other or other family members, the elf would leave them a holiday book to reward their good deeds. Daddy and I high-fived Santa's helper when we caught our little darlings being thoughtful toward each other months later! We also somehow ended up with a North Pole communicator, which the kids loved waking up to every morning in anticipation of what was going on in Christmas-town. They've really gotten smart and as early as Halloween this year, they started asking if they could intercom the elves to put in their Christmas wishes before the rush started and the color or size they wanted ran out.

There are other traditions that have continued and been passed down over the years as well. One activity that seems to top everyone's list is our annual Reindeer Run. This actually began with my parents when I was a little girl and it has meant so much to me over the years that I've made it a priority to do with my own family. This tradition starts with making some little inexpensive gift of love to share with family and friends. One year, we made glittered music paper shaped into wreaths; another year, we embellished clear, glass ornaments to be filled with written blessings from the year.

One of my favorite things to make and give, though, are Jam Sandwich cookies. I love these because they are easy, delicious, and involve the whole family. Once all the cookies are made, placed in little baggies, and tagged with a note of Christmas wishes, we all pile in the car at dark to hand deliver them to the families on our list. We make a quick stop for some hot-chocolate, find a radio station playing our favorite winter tunes, and start on our route. It's so much fun seeing our loved ones before the busyness of the season starts and wishing them tidings of great joy. Most of the time everyone is home but when they're not, we leave the cookies on their doorstep to find when they arrive later.

As the years have gone on, I think as many have come to look forward to our yearly stop as much as our family enjoys the reindeer run. The cookies aren't much but I want my children to enjoy the gift of giving, no matter how small, and I want to show them that caring for others is what Christmas is all about. After all, the greatest gift was the Christ-child given to us over 2,000 years ago. My mom taught us that gifts don't have to be expensive; just thoughtful and made with love from the heart.

P.S. A word of advice to all the moms: insist that you be the driver and make your husband and kids deliver the cookies. This helps keep the visits short and sweet so you can make it to everyone on your list ☺

Tasha Wilks was born in Colorado but moved to Texas when she was a young girl. It was there she got saved and became an active member in her church. She later graduated with honors from the University of North Texas and pursued her dream of becoming an educator. Her passion is to inspire children to become life-long learners. Currently, she resides in Denton, TX working as a reading interventionist in the same school district she grew up in. Tasha is joyously married to her husband Jeremy, has 2 children (Grayson and McKenzie), and is expecting a new baby in April. A full-time mom and educator, she is thrilled and humbled to be published for the very first time.

"Give a man a fish and you feed him for a day. Teach a man to fish and you feed him for a lifetime." – Ancient Chinese Proverb

Then he looked and behold,
there was at his head a bread cake baked on hot stones,
and a jar of water.
So he ate and drank and lay down again.

1 Kings 19:6

Jam Sandwich Cookies

Ingredients:

- 2 cups flour
- ½ teaspoon baking powder
- ½ teaspoon salt
- 12 tablespoons unsalted butter (at room temperature)
- 1 cup granulated sugar
- 1 egg
- ½ teaspoon vanilla
- ¾ cup confectioners sugar
- 1 cup seedless raspberry jam

Directions:

In a medium bowl, whisk flour, baking powder and salt.

With an electric mixer, beat butter and granulated sugar for about 3 minutes.

Beat in egg and vanilla. Gradually add flour mixtures.

Refrigerate 1 hour.

Using a large, heart shaped cookie cutter, cut out all of the cookie dough (to use for the bottom). Using a smaller heart-shaped cookie cutter, cut out a center heart of half the cookies (to use for the top).

Bake at 375 degrees for 8-10 minutes. Spread jam on the large heart and sandwich with the smaller, framed heart (to allow the jam to show through).

Enjoy!

So when they got out on the land,
they saw a charcoal fire already laid and fish placed on it,
and bread.

John 21:9 (NASB)

Discover WHO You Are and WHOSE You Are

How do you feel about yourself most days? Do you feel confident, self-assured, empowered, and ready to tackle the world? Or do you feel less than, undeserving, ill-equipped, and insufficient?

How we feel about ourselves plays a critical role in our overall success, and negative feelings can cause us to sell ourselves short and impede our ability to reach our highest potential. We may say things or act in ways that suggest we are anything short of capable and effective, and we develop a tendency to:

- Quickly dismiss compliments
- Feel like we have nothing to contribute or offer
- Allow others to seize opportunities ahead of us
- Worry about what others will think of us
- Procrastinate as a result of fear of failure

Thankfully, there is a solution. A Divine and Biblical solution for embracing our role as Daughter of the King.

Join me at
http://hissideofthelookingglass.com/introductory-offer/
to learn more.

Woman of Worth Affirmation

I know who I am and I am a woman of worth.
I can see how God sees me and I am valuable.
I am a daughter of the Most High King.
I am created in His image.
I am the work of His Hand.
He knows everything about me and I trust Him
to complete this good work in me.
I am dearly loved, His treasured possession,
and set apart for a noble purpose.
I am an heir to His Throne
with a divine destiny to fulfill.
By His Grace, I pledge to be
all He wants me to be, that I might be a good
representation of the One who created me.
I am special, unique, and important -
to God and those He puts in my path.
I can do all things
through Him who strengthens me.
He has a plan for me.
Therefore, I will jealously guard my mind
from anything that would defile this knowledge,
and I will glorify Jesus Christ.

He redeems me from death
and crowns me with love and tender mercies.
He fills my life with good things.
My youth is renewed like the eagle's!

Psalm 103:4-5 (NLT)

How You Can Help

Did you enjoy this book? Please help spread the word!

One way is to post a comment about it on Facebook and other social media forums, inviting your friends to have a look. Here's a simple message you can use:

> Just finished reading this book, *Becoming Women of Worth: Stories of Sugar & Spice and Recipes for the Holidays,* and I can't tell you how inspiring it was! I can't wait to try out some of the recipes in this book. And, I felt great comfort knowing I'm in the company of so many other wonderful women. It's a MUST READ!

Here are some other easy ways to help:

- Tell your colleagues and friends about this book; talk it up over coffee, during phone conversations, at gatherings, etc.

- Order a copy of the book for a friend.

- Post an honest review of this book on Amazon.

- Use this book as a book study with a small group.

And, thank you for your support!

FREE Confidence-Building Exercises for Writers

What we think about ourselves plays a critical role in our overall success, and negative thoughts can cause us to sell ourselves short and impede our ability to reach our highest potential. We may say things or act in ways that suggest we are anything short of capable and effective. This can also be bad news for us as writers because we may develop a tendency to:

- Procrastinate in submitting guest blog posts
- Use perfectionism as an excuse to not submit a book proposal for publication
- Allow others to seize publication or networking opportunities ahead of us
- Fear no one will want to read what we've written

Sound familiar? Download these SIX writing exercises designed to help you practice your writing craft while building confidence.

http://hissideofthelookingglass.com/writing-exercises/

About Kristen Clark

I am a creature of habit; I love routines. And one routine I have is the morning practice of standing in front of our bathroom mirror to get ready for the day. I brush my teeth in front of the mirror. I style my hair in front of the mirror. I put on my makeup in front of the mirror. I get dressed in front of the mirror. I put on my jewelry and finishing touches in front of the mirror. Finally, I check myself in the mirror before I head out to greet the world.

Some days I really like what I see in the mirror. Some days I'm not all that thrilled with what I see, but I consider this progress because there was a time in my life when a day didn't go by that I didn't like what I saw.

During much of my life, when I looked in the mirror I saw inadequacy. I thought I wasn't good enough, smart enough, pretty enough, funny enough… fill in the blank; I wasn't enough of it! I compared myself to other people and always believed I didn't measure up. I often had difficulty finding my own self-worth, and I let other people define my value. I suffered from low self-esteem and my greatest fear was that I would never amount to anything worthwhile, that I held no significant value.

I was afraid no one would want me or love me just as I was. My parents didn't instill this in me; it was simply what I chose to see. At the end of the day, I didn't like my reflection, and my actions and words showed I didn't like my reflection.

Unfortunately, I suffered from misperception of self. I failed to see the truth and reality of who I was. Instead, I saw myself through distorted lenses. One day, a woman at church said to me, "Kristen, I wish you could learn to see yourself as God sees you because you are amazing."

I didn't know what that meant – to see myself as God sees me – but I had lived in enough pain for so long that I wanted to find out. So, I embarked on a journey and began the process of reprogramming my brain to align with what God's Word says about who I am in Him, and I began to understand my noble purpose. As a result, I want to share my experience, strength, and hope in an effort to help other women shed their perception of self and become Women of Worth.

When not speaking or writing on *this* subject, I speak and write on living with gratitude and writing for publication. My articles have appeared in numerous online journals and magazines, while my inspirational short stories have been published in several volumes of *Chicken Soup for the Soul.*

I'm also a member of the American Association of Christian Counselors and my book, *Becoming a Woman of Worth: Creating a More Confident You,* won a gold medal in the 2014 Readers' Favorite International Book Award Contest in the category of Christian Biblical Counseling.

Additionally, I have over twenty years of experience working in small business and corporate America, and a wealth of practical business knowledge. I have successfully held positions in Sales, Management, Strategy and Planning, Marketing, and Executive Communications.

Finally, I'm an editor and publisher with a huge heart for helping others write and publish their inspirational short story. For more information on our publishing services, visit www.AmericanMuttPress.com.

For more information about my other speaking topics, or to hire me to speak to your church, company, or organization, feel free to visit www.kristenclark.org or email Kristen@kristenclark.org.

For more information, please visit:

- www.HisSideoftheLookingGlass.com
- www.BecomingaWomanofWorth.com
- www.LivingwithGratitude.com
- www.KristenClark.org
- www.AllThingsButterflies.com
- www.AmericanMuttPress.com

Becoming a Woman of Worth:
Creating a More Confident You

By Kristen Clark

Available on Amazon.com and
BarnesandNoble.com

Becoming Women of Worth:
Stories of Hope & Faith

By Kristen Clark

Available on Amazon.com and
BarnesandNoble.com

Becoming Women of Worth:
Stories of Trauma & Triumph

By Kristen Clark

Available on Amazon.com and
BarnesandNoble.com

KRISTEN CLARK

How to Write & Publish Your
Inspirational Short Story

By Kristen Clark and
Lawrence J. Clark, PhD

Available on Amazon.com and
BarnesandNoble.com

CPSIA information can be obtained
at www.ICGtesting.com
Printed in the USA
LVHW052217220123
737736LV00013B/828